BOOK OF TRXTH

God Gives You Free-will. The Devil Gives You Bad Choices

By

James Dubose

writing as TRXTH

ISBN 979-8-9868829-0-1

James Dubose

onetrxth@gmail.com

Preface

There are some who are reluctant to follow the Bible because they believe the story to be fictional, a fairy tale, intended for children. This depiction, although inaccurate, may have some truth. The Bible is written in such a way that you can teach it to children. There may be a couple of reasons why this is done. The wisdom that the Bible is trying to convey is in opposition to the information your enemy wants you to have about God and the world. The Bible's presentation has allowed it to become the world's most published book with an estimated distribution totaling 5 billion. That is a victory for those who wrote the Bible.

The first page(s) of the Bible provides the author's key—it's the Creator's design. This design is consistent, and you'll begin to notice that the Creator does not confuse the 'Word' or the 'Design.' If you don't understand the first pages of the Bible, you will not be able to make sense of any of the books of the Bible.

The Bible also has to contend with time, man's greatest obstacle. This is why it uses symbolism so that even though the meanings and uses of words change, what the symbols represent and their meanings don't. The story has to be written in such a way that a reader millennia later can understand it. This is why the Bible uses symbolism and metaphors, those things that exist now, that will also exist thousands of years from now. Today and a millennium from now a tree and a snake will represent what they represent today. What the Bible is communicating to the reader is God's design is the Rosetta Stone.

Presenting it as a story allows the reader to teach it to a child, and as the child matures the teacher can then graduate the level of the child's understanding. The problem we have is that we tend to stay in the children's story mode of teaching and understanding the Bible. The Bible has layers of understanding and complexity, and every word is important to the story and to the understanding. This is why in the past you could be killed for distorting or changing a word in the Bible. When we get to a point where we understand what the Bible is trying to teach, then and only then will we be able to understand why this is a justifiable punishment.

Another reason it is written this way is that history has proven that knowledge comes and goes. The knowledge from those who have created great structures in our past has been lost, but it is the stories that transcend time. It is only important biblical stories that have survived. As man's knowledge wanes, an important tool for passing on knowledge is storytelling or oral traditions. It's also important for those who may become oppressed to be able to continue to share with future generations wisdom that may be forbidden to be written in their presence. Christians past and present have been persecuted and incarcerated for being in possession of the written Word of God, the Bible.

Today, there are at least 50 countries that do not allow possession of the Bible without penalty, the harshest of penalties being given by North Korea. In North Korea possession of the Bible is a capital offense and includes the possibility of punishment for family members of the offender as well. The question is why would any country punish or ban a book if it's simply a children's story?

What we have failed to do as biblical followers is excavate the understanding the story is trying to communicate. The story as told is intended for growth. Once the reader has matured, he already knows the people, places, and events that have taken place. Now it's time to broaden the scope of what's being communicated. This will explain why many people who have read the Bible can testify that at different stages in life, the Bible itself will bring greater clarity to what's written.

Contents

Introduction

The History of the World: It Doesn't Have to Happen Again

Has there ever been a time in human history when there was no threat to the children of God? Since the creation of the world, there has been a battle going on between good and evil, light and darkness. But our experiences in life shape how we view the world. As I look back on my own life, I can remember a world that was mostly good. I remember a world that was friendlier than the world is today, at least in my tiny corner. There was no doubt horrific evil going on but not in my neighborhood in the poor black area of the west end of Cincinnati.

But that same neighborhood today is a victim of "progress." Are things getting worse all over? The answer is *yes, things always get worse* over time. That is the cycle, and we are nearing the end of one. If you look back in history, you will see that this has happened many times since the creation of the world. The cycle is always the same: Men who follow God and his Law set out to live in the world as 'his' children. Other men who do not follow God and his Law and hate the truth, set out to destroy the children of God. As long as the men who obey the Creator, follow his Law, honor God and obey, they prosper and the world prospers. As they successfully drive out the darkness, the world will continue to produce and create life according to the blueprint of God.

But at some point, the evil one, the serpent comes in with the lies, the temptation, and "knowledge" that is tempting to the children of God. Soon the children of God forgot how to recognize the men of the darkness. They are unable to stay separate from them. They are curious, tempted by their lusts, and taken over by them. Adam was the first to succumb.

Eventually, God, having seen the failure of his children, must intervene, and he does so. Once, it was a great flood. Another time, it was the scrambling of language and the creation of the nations. It was the calling of the vicarious man, Moses, and then the destruction of that day's superpower of darkness, Egypt, Egypt's gods, and its Pharaoh.

Those are some of the major ones, but the same cycle has played out in every society that ever existed, from the smallest tribe to the largest world power, and it is happening right now across the globe and in America. What will it look like for God to intervene in the coming days? You might be tempted to pray for that, but you would be naive. God's design is for his children to do what they were created to do, produce, multiply, and subdue the world.

My Aim for this Book

Because we are at war, a war of good vs. evil, my great burden for this book is to change the world by changing the way God's children view the world, removing the darkness, the forces of evil in our homes, our neighborhoods, our cities, states, nations, and our globe. I will bring clarity and answer your "why" questions—the questions you were asking last week, May 24, 2022(as of this writing) when a crazy person shot 21 people, most of them children, at a school in Texas. These are the questions you were asking when Putin invaded Ukraine, on February 24, 2022. When BLM started a movement and then broke the hearts of their followers with their corruption. When you opened the news this morning and read about the things people are capable of doing to one another when you observe evil. I'm going to answer your questions.

If after reading this you don't see the World and the Word differently, if you don't see your fellow man as an extension of your biological family and have a newfound respect for the earth beneath your feet...then I've failed.

Contrary to what we've been taught, we're not waiting on God, God is waiting on us. He who has created time has an eternity, Man does not.

I don't expect anyone to blindly follow what I've written, what is required is that you check for yourself what I've presented and then decide. What I'm sharing is not an opinion, but an understanding that can be proven true or false.

But be warned, to have Truth is to have responsibility. I'm going to give you the Truth, but also a way forward, a call to action, to arms. And I will attempt to paint a picture of what it could be like if the children of God heeded the call of God to live in his kingdom on earth "as it is in heaven." Where do we start? We start with the Bible.

Part One

The Basics

Chapter 1

The Rosetta Stone Is God's Design, Genesis 1-3

Many people love the Bible and claim its authority over their lives. They rightly call it the Word of God. Today, Christians everywhere love the New Testament and the meek and mild Christ presented in its pages. But in order to understand the New Testament, you have to understand the Old Testament. The Bible is to be studied and every word is important and meaningful.

And it is the first pages of the Old Testament which are the key to the Bible. Genesis 1, 2, and 3 provide the tools necessary to make sense of the rest of Scripture. There are no contradictions in the Bible. If there is anything in the Bible that appears to be a contradiction, this is a misunderstanding. These misunderstandings are born out of the lies we're taught about the world. The lies we are taught divide and confuse. Where there is division and confusion, there's also the influence of the devil.

The Old Testament and the New Testament are two sides of the same truth. You don't have to believe the people are real or that the events actually happened. What's important is what these biblical stories of Moses are trying to teach. Even if you don't believe they happened, you will believe they are true.

The aim of this is to give an understanding of the purpose of the Bible and to give the reader the tools needed to answer any questions they may have. Many scholars have written about whether the events actually happened or not. It is not my aim to debate this, but rather to see that the truth is written in the following pages. Discovering the intent of the most published and read book in history is my aim. What will become clear is how consistent God is with his design. Evil is anything that attempts to deviate from that design or confuse the understanding of God. This is anything that is not of God. A true understanding of the Bible should bring forth clarity regarding who God is and what God's people are supposed to be doing.

One of the most intriguing things about the Bible is that our understanding is always personal. What other book is like that? I've heard it said that once you truly begin to read the Bible, the Bible begins to read you. Each person will come to his own conclusion as to what the Bible is trying to communicate. This happens so consistently that there are thousands of different denominations that are based on the Bible. Christianity is divided into myriad sects, all claiming the authority of Scripture for their theological variations.

Most people have an understanding that began with what they were taught by their mother and father, but what also influences them is *how* they were taught. Those who educate us about the world influence our understanding of who God is. This is important because the Word of God and the world created by God reveals the truth about God, and how both are presented influence us tremendously.

The Word and the world are complements of one another and together they present only one truth, one God. Rather than being told who that one God is, you will be given the truth to discern for yourself who He is. To this point, you may have been presented with many gods or many ideas about God, but you have yet to receive the Truth of the one God. There are those who have this truth, but only present certain elements of it in order to deceive and manipulate the masses, keeping us asleep and disconnected from one another and from God. The story of Adam and Eve, which is about deception, is just one illustration of what will happen to the masses. The Bible is of crucial importance to our everyday lives but has been used as a weapon against us.

When we first take a look into the Bible what we see is the foundation for the relationship between man and God. God establishes order first, God, Man then beast. He then gives us the law and the consequences for disobeying this law. This law is also consistent with the relationship we have with the world. If the beast had the free will to decide whether to disobey the one law it was given: to be fruitful and multiply, it would inevitably lead to the extinction of that animal. Regardless of the conditions of the world the beast, fowl, and fish do not deviate. The simplest understanding is that there are always outside pressures to reduce wildlife populations whether man-made, natural, or predatory. These same conditions exist for man. This is our first clue in determining who is God.

The Incontestable Bible

Before God created man He created Heaven and Earth and all the things on Earth. Before the first words of the Bible were written by Moses, the laws of God were already established. The laws of God are contained and maintained by those things 'He' has created. What makes man special is free will. Unlike other creatures, only man can disobey God.

The Bible forbids adding, removing, or making any changes.

> **Ye shall not add unto the word which I command you, neither shall ye diminish ought from it, that ye may keep the commandments of the LORD your God which I command you. (Deut 4:2 KJV)**

My intent is not to add unto the Word, but to clarify what the Word says. We suffer because we fail to grasp the true meaning of the Bible, and what God aims to communicate through the Bible. Man has come up with many arguments against the Word of God. One of such arguments is that the Bible was written and manipulated by man. Others point to the seeming contradictions in the Bible and question whether any of the events actually occurred. The truth is that there aren't any biblical contradictions. One can misunderstand what they've read, and that is surely what is happening when it seems there is a contradiction, but this simply requires biblical clarity.

Others say, "No one can truly know what God wants." This is not true. The problem is that whoever is your teacher controls how you see the world. Evidence of God has been right in front of us the entire time. Paul in Romans 1 explains that all men know there is a God simply by observing.

> [18] For the wrath of God is revealed from heaven against all ungodliness and unrighteousness of men, who by their unrighteousness suppress the truth. [19] *For what can be known about God is plain to them because God has shown it to them.* [20] For his invisible attributes, namely, his eternal power and divine nature, *have been clearly perceived, ever since the creation of the world, in the things that have been made.* So they are *without excuse.*
>
> [21] For although they knew God, they did not honor him as God or give thanks to him, but they became futile in their thinking, and their foolish hearts were darkened. [22] Claiming to be wise, they became fools, [23] and exchanged the glory of the immortal God for images resembling mortal man and birds and animals and creeping things.
>
> [24] Therefore God gave them up in the lusts of their hearts to impurity, to the dishonoring of their bodies among themselves, 25 because they exchanged the truth about God for a lie and worshiped and served the creature rather than the Creator, who is blessed forever! Amen. (Emphasis added)

We'll discuss this further below, but for now, let us go back to the very first pages of the Bible. Genesis 1:24-25 says,

> [24] And God said, Let the earth bring forth the living creature after his kind, cattle, and creeping thing, and beast of the earth after his kind: and it was so. [25] And God made the beast of the earth after his kind, and cattle after their kind, and everything

that creepeth upon the earth after his kind: and God saw that it was good. (Gen KJV)

The incontestable Bible shows God's design. God gave Adam the command not to eat the tree *because* Adam had free will. God didn't have to give commands to the other creatures. They do not have free will and must obey. All God's creatures behave in a way that maintains balance and allows Man to live. They behave like machines, and they do not sin as long as man does not interfere through breeding and domestication. Have you ever wondered why birds fly south for the winter or bears hibernate? Or why some beasts obey God's dietary law and are herbivores. They cannot disobey God who has ordered them to do so.

This incontestable truth is how we can reconcile what we believe with what is true. The incontestable Bible also gives us insight into other things. God creates all types of birds, different types of cats, and different kinds of fishes, yet we mistakenly believe there is only one type of man among us. God's design is very consistent. Although we have many types of cats: lions, tigers, and cheetahs they do not interbreed. Of course, the only exception is when man interferes. Different Bears—Brown, Polar, and Asian Black Bear do not mix. These are examples of *segregation* in God's Law.

I'm sure some would argue that of course some of these animals don't interbreed, because they're not in close proximity to one another, such as the Tiger which does not exist in Africa and the Lion which has a very small presence in a small region of Asia.

This only proves more of how God intended us to live. This is why the Bible states that these horrible things that will happen to Man will happen in diverse places. God has separated us by vast deserts, oceans, and seas. God intended for Man to live among his kind, separate from the Beast and those who represent him.

Thou Shalt Not Kill

There is another law presented by the incontestable Bible, which is "thou shalt not kill." I believe this law is the most misunderstood, but looking at how God has created the animal kingdom can shed some light here. What makes this law hard to understand is that we believe we are all God's children, but we are not. Put another way, "Thou shalt not kill another child of God." Other creatures, God has made: killer whales, piranhas, crocodiles—these animals are absolute killers. But it is interesting that they rarely attack one another within their kind. They are able to exist among one another, but they do not prey on each other.

> **11 And it came to pass in those days, when Moses was grown, that he went out unto his brethren, and looked on their burdens: and he spied an Egyptian smiting an Hebrew, one of his brethren.**
>
> **12 And he looked this way and that way, and when he saw that there was no man, he slew the Egyptian and hid him in the sand. (Ex 2:11-12 KJV)**

Consider that when Moses killed the Egyptian he was looked upon favorably by God, although he has supposedly committed murder. Most Christians will say, "God forgave him for it." But this is not the case. In God's eyes, there was nothing to forgive, because the Bible is not about love; it is about war. God is a lot of things, and one of those things is a commander of armies, who gives commandments and a standing order to his children to "subdue the earth." This requires his children to kill the Beast and anyone who represents the Beast. Killing a beast is not murder, killing a child of God is murder. To make this point clear, the verse says the Egyptian was smiting his brethren. If we were all children of God, the Egyptian would also be the brother of Moses, but he is not. The truth in its entirety is that we are all God's creation, but we are not all children of God. More will follow in this chapter 3.

The Bible is about the world, and the more we understand God's design of the world, the more we will understand the Bible and how we must live in it. I did not start with a desire to understand the Bible, but my desire to understand the world led me back to the Bible and a hunger to know it.

The Bible isn't the only thing directing us to look at the design, man-made wonders like the Great Pyramid is as well directing us. Every civilization before us has tried to warn us of what's ahead. That's why we have so many ancient writings that include Biblical stories.

Time for man is not linear but cyclical, we have seasons for Man that last thousands of years. Mega structures like the Great Pyramid are trying to send a message to us from the past. We can infer from looking at the Great Pyramid that it was intended to stand for thousands of years. It is also noted that the GP has no writing. What can be concluded from this is that they don't want you to focus on what's written but on the design, God's design. It also wasn't used for burial. They wouldn't have used it for burial because they wouldn't have wanted to focus your attention on death.

The math that's encoded in the structure is the math that reveals God's design. The structure stands at the exact center of all land masses exactly where the longest lines of latitude and longitude intersect. It's also aligned with true north, which it uses in its design, the metric unit of measure, and many other celestial alignments and mathematical truths that were only discovered in our most recent history.

This is yet another message from our ancestors that the truth of God is in the design. The amount of labor and material sourced to warn future generations is a testament to the importance of understanding the laws of God.

The Great Pyramid's design doesn't rely upon faith but on understanding, the understanding that we do not have today, an understanding that proved they knew if it was built accordingly it would absolutely stand the test of time. And it has.

This is the same understanding we need in order to ensure that God's Kingdom will stand. The OT warns that we are "destroyed for lack of knowledge," (Hos 4:6), not because of lack of faith. Knowing is the other side of faith and just another duality. Faith is believing in what can't be proven. Truth is knowing what your actions will produce.

What can also be said by observing the Great Pyramid is that only great civilizations can build great temples. This suggests that there was a time when the children of God flourished. There are temples around the world. But what happens is those born under freedom typically don't have the same respect that those who fought for it have.

What can then be said by a civilization that builds Great Walls? Walls have always been a marker for communism. It is a testament that man has continually dealt with that which is in opposition to God. God's people form alliances against evil. Walls represent division. The shield of God's children is the Creator.

The Creator wants you to have "truth," which is why his design is so consistent. The world is in the condition it's in because the satanic gave us our religion, our news, and our education. They control our money, our systems of government, and the media.

What you'll notice is at the fall of these past civilizations there is an obsession with death, such as with the Egyptians and their book of the dead and their necropolis, and the Mayans with their child sacrifices.

Structure

As you continue to read the Bible it establishes structure. God, man, then every living thing. The woman isn't mentioned intentionally, because at this point they are still one. God establishes his authority over all things by being the Creator first and later by commanding.

> **And God blessed them, and God said unto them, Be fruitful, and multiply, and replenish the earth, and subdue it: and have dominion over the fish of the sea, and over the fowl of the air, and over every living thing that moveth upon the earth. (Gen 1:28 KJV)**

God commands the creatures when He tells them to be fruitful and multiply. God establishes man's authority by giving dominion over all things and the responsibility to subdue the earth. The Bible refers to men as God's children which also further establishes this structure. God over man and God's children over Earth.

The structure is important in establishing authority. This structure is found throughout God's design. In nature, we can observe structures with lions, bees, ants, and primates. These animals and others have a very structured hierarchy and are examples of animals that are created after 'His' kind. The hyena would be an example of those creatures created after 'their' kind, whereas the female is the head and the male is submissive. The hyena and the lion are natural enemies. It is important to note that in this structure you have order and opposition to this order.

These systems and subsystems are all interrelated, which is why as we continue exploring the Bible, we will see that understanding duality is important to understanding the Bible and God's laws. Duality is consistent in God's design and we'll continue to add layers to this understanding.

The animals that God has placed among us are no different than the teaching aids we provide our own children. He has given us all things so that we may study the design and learn from it. Man's advancement requires nothing more than replicating what God has already perfected in nature, whether that is flight, electricity, light, or communication.

The Word of God is in the design, if you want to understand Scripture it takes nothing more than observing the world around you.

Principles of Symbolism

God never breathed life into the beast, therefore they don't have a soul.

There is much detail in the Bible, and it is not difficult to gloss over the fine points that are important to the message. In the beginning, God gave the beast, fowl, and fish one commandment, and he gave man two. Both man and beast were given the command to be fruitful and multiply, but only man was commanded to not eat of the Tree of Knowledge. This command, along with the authority of dominion and the power to subdue, helps to establish how man is created in the image of God. The animals that God created are true to God's design, behave accordingly, and do not deviate. They are hardwired to obey God's law. The man instead is given a soul and free will.

> **And the LORD God formed man of the dust of the ground, and breathed into his nostrils the breath of life; and man became a living soul (Gen 2:7 KJV).**

The first two commands God gave us were to be fruitful and multiply, and not to eat of the tree of knowledge. The very thing your enemy doesn't want you to have is the truth and babies. What has become evident is the more "knowledgeable" we become, the fewer children we produce and the further we move away from God. This is why God warns us to not eat of the tree of knowledge. Knowledge severs our relationship with God. The problem with knowledge is that knowledge is not equal to truth and when presented with knowledge, like Eve, you won't know the difference. 2 Timothy 3:7 says, "Ever learning, and never able to come to the knowledge of the truth" (KJV).

War

Later in chapter 3, I'll show why you must accept that we're not all God's children. Here I want you to understand that because of this, you have to accept that the Bible is about war. The war that the Bible is introducing is a war of deception. We typically only think of war as two nations in a physical battle with one another, but this war by deception is what the story of Adam and Eve introduced. The serpent introduced the deception and that deception produced death. God warned Adam and Eve, and they disobeyed. Their story is intended to be a warning for future generations of the children of God to not make the mistakes that they made.

Adam and Eve's disobedience to God isn't only about their decision to choose life or death, but it's about everyone's decision to do the same. Though the notion is popular among Christians and biblical followers that Adam and Eve condemned the world to suffer, this simply isn't true. You must grasp that Adam and Eve didn't condemn all of humanity because of their choices. Everyone is born with the option to choose for him or herself Life or Death. The war for your soul is to beguile you so that you make the wrong decision.

> *"I am the punishment of God...If you had not committed great sins, God would not have sent a punishment like me upon you."*
>
> **- Genghis Khan**

This statement by Ghenghis Khan is accurate, there is a point to the laws God has given man. He didn't do it just to have a display of power or control over us. We were given these laws so that we may accomplish the very instructions he gave us to subdue the earth. Also, if you can observe the design, you will notice *that the punishment for breaking the laws of God is in the design.* This is illustrated with the death of Abel in Genesis, Abel did nothing wrong, but he suffered the consequences of the decisions of his mother and father. God explains this when giving his laws to Moses.

> **Keeping mercy for thousands, forgiving iniquity and transgression and sin, and that will by no means clear the guilty; *visiting the iniquity of the fathers upon the children, and upon the children's children, unto the third and to the fourth generation.* (Ex 34:7 KJV emphasis added)**

The Tree of Knowledge of Good and Evil

In chapter 2 we will discuss the duality of God's design and the perfect balance he has created on the earth. Man was created to "subdue the earth." This meant that he was supposed to keep the world under God's authority. Adam was *given* authority. It was delegated. He failed.

Free Will

But can the children of the Lord subdue the earth? Can those who God made in his image and called very good take back the precious ground given up to the darkness? The answer is found in God's statement from the beginning. This is an "if-then" statement, and God is fond of such causal relationships.

> **[15] The Lord God took the man and put him in the garden of Eden to work it and keep it. [16] And the Lord God commanded the man, saying, "You may surely eat of every tree of the garden, [17] but of the tree of the knowledge of good and evil you shall not eat, for in the day that you eat of it you shall surely die." (Gen 2:15-17)**

But in another way, he says to his child, "*if* you eat only of the trees that I have commanded you to eat, *then* you will live and not die." These causal statements all throughout the Bible are always about one thing, choice, and not just any choice, but the *choice to live or die.* God repeats this statement again and again.

> **If you are willing and obedient, you shall eat the good of the land. (Isa 1:19 ESV)**

> **For the people of Israel walked forty years in the wilderness, until all the nation, the men of war who came out of Egypt, perished because they did not obey the voice of the Lord; the Lord swore to them that he would not let them see the land that the Lord had sworn to their fathers to give to us, a land flowing with milk and honey. (Josh 5:6 ESV)**

> **And if you faithfully obey the voice of the Lord your God, being careful to do all his commandments that I command you today, the Lord your God will set you high above all the nations of the earth. (Deut 28:1 ESV)**

> **You shall walk in all the way that the Lord your God has commanded you, that you may live, and that it may go well with you, and that you may live long in the land that you shall possess. (Deut 5:33 ESV)**

> **And all these blessings shall come upon you and overtake you if you obey the voice of the Lord your God. (Deut 28:8 ESV)**

> **See, I am setting before you today a blessing and a curse: the blessing if you obey the commandments of the Lord your God, which I command you today, and the curse, if you do not obey the commandments of the Lord your God, but turn aside from the way that I am commanding you today, to go after other gods that you have not known. (Deut 11:26-28 ESV)**

The devil can't take your free will unless you relinquish God's protection by disobeying God. Even then he can really only trick you into thinking you don't have free will. If you have given yourself to the devil, then you have given over your will. Even this you have done as an act of free will.

When we think of "knowledge" such as that gained by Eve from disobedience, one such piece of "knowledge" is that of determinism. It is an error committed by both believers and nonbelievers. But it is sophistry. All such knowledge is sophistry.

Choose Life

What makes God's people special is that they choose Life, and to choose Life is to obey God's law. Man, Satan, or even God doesn't take away your free will. Upon birth, God gives you Life and Liberty. During your life, the devil tempts you with death and slavery. If you choose to go against God's design for the world, you relinquish your special status. If you choose, for instance, homosexuality, interracial marriage (which we will discuss in a later chapter), abortion, or refusal to bear children and to live as a common man, it's permissible under man's law, but you relinquish God's protection when you forego God's law.

Each person chooses. I have seven children, and I know the choices that I would like them to make. Like most parents, I advise them. The Bible refers to us as children, and we are. The Old Testament is trying to advise God's children. When our children don't make the right choices, we don't stop loving them, but we understand the danger in which they are putting themselves.

The laws that are outlined in the Old Testament are there so that we may enjoy God's kingdom as he intended. If you are going to be a king or a queen, you must relinquish those choices that are available to the common man. The king and queen have certain privileges but they must relinquish certain freedoms. God has established his children as rulers over the Earth, by giving *his* children dominion over all things. In order for God's children to maintain their kingdom, they must keep God's commandments.

> **14 When thou art come unto the land which the Lord thy God giveth thee, and shalt possess it, and shalt dwell therein, and shalt say, I will set a king over me, like as all the nations that are around about me;**
>
> **15 Thou shalt in any wise set him king over thee, whom the Lord thy God shall choose: one from among thy brethren shalt thou set king over thee: thou mayest not set a stranger over thee, which is not thy brother.**

> 16 ***But he shall not multiply horses to himself*, nor cause the people to return to Egypt, to the end that he should multiply horses: forasmuch as the Lord hath said unto you, Ye shall henceforth return no more that way.**
>
> 17 ***Neither shall he multiply wives to himself, that his heart turn not away: neither shall he greatly multiply to himself silver and gold.***
>
> 18 **And it shall be, when he sitteth upon the throne of his kingdom, *that he shall write him a copy of this law* in a book out of that which is before the priests the Levites:**
>
> 19 **And it shall be with him, and he shall read therein all the days of his life: that *he may learn to fear the Lord his God, to keep all the words of this law and these statutes, to do them:***
>
> 20 **That his heart be not lifted up above his brethren, and that he turn not aside from the commandment, to the right hand, or to the left: to the end that he may prolong his days in his kingdom, he, and his children, in the midst of Israel. (Deut 17:14-20 KJV emphasis added)**

This is what God's people do not understand. Too much "freedom" leads to slavery. It's the old adage, give a man enough rope he'll hang himself. Our freedoms exist, but they exist within the laws of God. So here we have a *seeming* contradiction. We have free will that cannot be taken away, but we must take it away ourselves. We must use our will to give up our will. We must use our freedom to chain ourselves to God and to God's laws. Francis Bacon, English philosopher, statesman, and one of the fathers of the scientific method, said, "Nature, to be commanded, must be obeyed." Bacon was trying to say that no matter how free your will is, you do not have the freedom to break the laws of nature, the laws of truth, which are the laws of God. He was saying that if we submit to its laws, we can operate freely within it. If you will submit to the laws of gravity, then you can learn to manipulate it and fly. If you will submit to the laws of mathematics, then you can solve all manner of practical problems—building bridges, ships, cars, skyscrapers, and Great Pyramids. If you break these laws, they will break you. 1 + 1 will always be equal to 2, and to deny it is to court death. Reality is real. Existence exists. A thing is what it is, and is not what it is not.

But on top of God's laws of physics and nature, he has given us the book of the law in the Bible. Some of these seem less obvious to us as to why he gave them. Adam may well have understood the reason for the law of gravity that said, "Don't jump out of that tree," while not comprehending the one from the mouth of God which said, "Don't eat of that tree." And yet, he was beholden to use his free will to obey, rather than disobey.

Consider these:

> **"Thou shalt not sow thy vineyard with divers seeds: lest the fruit of thy seed which thou hast sown, and the fruit of thy vineyard, be defiled" (Deut 22:9 KJV).**

> **"Divers weights, and divers measures, both of them are alike abominations to the Lord" (Prov 20:10 KJV).**

Divers(e) weights and divers(e) measures are an abomination because it is in opposition to what our God represents, truth and honesty. God also represents segregation and total consistency. The scales must be balanced because God will always balance the scales.

The prohibition against divers(e) seeds is harder to understand, but crucial. Again, our God is a God of law and order. Diversity is in opposition to God, and it's also what's currently being pushed in our society—multiculturalism. But God takes great pains to separate. He has made things, each *of its kind.* Animals will only crossbreed in a lab under human supervision. In the wild, they know better. If divers(e) seeds are allowed to grow and weeds are sewn in among them, the fruit will be choked out and strange hybrids less nutritious will be the result.

The Satanists understand there is no order where there is no law. Diversity means anything for everybody and everybody for anything. Moral judgment is cast aside, because, "Who am I to judge?" But God's creation suggests that order and law maintain life. It brings fruitfulness.

As we are all aware, man has the ability to decide what is right, what is wrong, what is law, and what isn't, and even whether there is a God or not. This only happens by disobeying the law, the prohibition of eating the Tree of Knowledge. Just like the children we are in the eyes of God, regardless of age, as we become more knowledgeable we begin to deviate from God's law, meaning we become more sinful. The problem God has with knowledge is that it is not equal to truth. The serpent gave Eve knowledge but he didn't give her the truth.

> **And the serpent said unto the woman, Ye shall not surely die (Gen 3:4 KJV).**

> **Thou shalt not bow down thyself to them, nor serve them: for I the LORD thy God am a jealous God, visiting the iniquity of the fathers upon the children unto the third and fourth generation of them that hate me (Ex 20:5 KJV).**

It may appear harsh to punish the children for the decisions of the parents but understand, the children get their understanding of God and the world from their parents. Then parents take note, in order to correct our children we must chastise them. God is no different in parenting his earthly children. If no correction is given, then the parents and children have no incentive to change or seek a higher understanding. This also provides an understanding of how important children are. Children help us put into perspective a better understanding of God. Children are also an investment in the future, so anyone who would lead, or who would be followed by you should take seriously this investment. If a leader does not have children or even a lot of children, they shouldn't be trusted with our future.

In America, our military has what is called a UCMJ, Uniformed Code of Military Justice. It is also referred to as the "Bible" when introduced to new enlistees. Our children are God's new cadets, and you can give your new soldier God's law, which is the Tree of Life, or Man's Law, which is the Tree of Knowledge.

How to think of the New Testament (or alternative introduction to the NT

Galatians 3:23-29 (KJV) says,

> **23 But before faith came, we were kept under the law, shut up unto the faith which should afterwards be revealed. 24 Wherefore the law was our schoolmaster to bring us unto Christ, that we might be justified by faith. 25 But after that faith is come, we are no longer under a schoolmaster. 26 For ye are all the children of God by faith in Christ Jesus. 27 For as many of you as have been baptized into Christ have put on Christ. 28 There is neither Jew nor Greek, there is neither bond nor free, there is neither male nor female: for ye are all one in Christ Jesus. 29 And if ye be Christ's, then are ye Abraham's seed, and heirs according to the promise.**

This verse makes it clear. Before there was faith, there was the law. It also makes it clear that if you follow Christ, you are no longer special. You're neither Jew nor Gentile, slave or free, male or female; you're all oppressed and exploited commoners.

The Book Of The Ruling Class versus The Book Of The Common Class (or Communist Class)

The book of the ruling class is the OT, and the book of the common class is the NT. The OT gives the laws that are needed for a nation to maintain its sovereignty. No country or nation can maintain its freedoms or independence under NT teachings. In order to establish and maintain a nation, you must have law and order. Love is for the commoner. You also must be able to enforce these laws. Many of us have adopted the NT as our standard, but we don't maintain that standard in our homes. The laws that you are to have for your nation are to be consistent with the laws that are in your community and your home. Parents would not encourage their children to love their enemy or to turn the other cheek. Our government also shouldn't love its enemies or turn the other cheek. It is a weakness that invites attack.

The way to understand the Bible requires you to figure out who you are. These two books are not meant to be read or followed as one book. Each book will produce the results they were meant to produce. Every civilization before us has had both.

Each book, the Old Testament and the New Testament are two sides of the truth. If you want to maintain life, law, and rule, the Old Testament will produce this. If you want death, love, and the ability to endure oppression and slavery, the New Testament will help guide you through enduring that condition.

The war by deception only requires those who are represented in the OT to follow those who are represented in the NT. Once God's children elevate 'Love' over 'Law' that's a defeat for the children who the OT was written for.

> *When the missionaries came to Africa they had the Bible and we had the land. They said 'Let us pray.' We closed our eyes. When we opened them we had the Bible and they had the land.*
>
> – **Desmond Tutu**

The NT requires you to love your enemy and to turn the other cheek. You will not find these instructions in the OT. The OT deals with Life and the condition of your Life. The OT never promises Heaven. The Heaven that's promised in the NT requires Death.

The Bible is not a prophecy, but rather a warning of things that have already happened and will happen again. As parents, it is not necessary for us to have psychic abilities in order to warn our children of the results of certain behaviors. Children will often not heed the warnings of their parents, only to later learn after suffering why they should have listened. The OT is that warning from our parent, our Heavenly Father.

If you understand God's design, it becomes easy to understand what comes next. This is what the Bible is trying to reveal; it's trying to explain in a story its design. The OT is easy to follow in that it is simply "if this, then that." If you eat from the Tree of Knowledge, then you'll know death. If you break the covenant, then you'll know suffering. If you follow after other Gods, the Almighty will turn away from you, or even against you.

Leviticus 26:14-16, 24, 27-29 (KJV) says,

> **[14] But if ye will not hearken unto me, and will not do all these commandments; [15] And if ye shall despise my statutes, or if your soul abhor my judgments, so that ye will not do all my commandments, but that ye break my covenant: [16] I also will do this unto you; I will even appoint over you terror, consumption, and the burning ague, that shall consume the eyes, and cause sorrow of heart: and ye shall sow your seed in vain, for your enemies shall eat it.**
>
> **[24] Then will I also walk contrary unto you, and will punish you yet seven times for your sins.**
>
> **[27] And if ye will not for all this hearken unto me, but walk contrary unto me; [28] Then I will walk contrary unto you also in fury; and I, even I, will chastise you seven times for your**

sins. [29] And ye shall eat the flesh of your sons, and the flesh of your daughters shall ye eat.

The OT is actually warning you about the NT. What preceded the enslavement of Africans were NT teachings and the elevating of Jesus to God. What better way to subdue a people than by abusing and oppressing them then saying that it is godly to take it, and they will be rewarded in Heaven for doing so?

Laws of the Bible and the Laws of Nature

The OT laws are not arbitrary laws given to man simply to control his behavior for arbitrary reasons. The OT laws are actually about physics. Physics is the science of matter, energy, and its interactions. The word "physics" comes from the Greek word *physikos*, meaning the science of nature. The OT is the science of man. Once you understand God's design, it makes it relatively easy to understand what comes next.

Man is unique in all things God has created. Everything he has created has laws that govern its behavior. The laws that God has in place govern the universe, and these laws are what allow Man to live. If you somehow interrupt any of the systems or subsystems that God has set in place, life for man becomes harsh, and in some instances, unlivable.

So then the question is, what is disobedience? Disobedience is a sin. What is sin? Sin is a deviation from God's design, God's law. This is why the Bible begins with creation.

There are many men among us with knowledge of science and the laws that they must adhere to in order to execute certain functions or designs. What must be understood is that all things

God created have laws to govern them. We have laws of physics, laws of flight, and laws of motion, just to name a few. What modern man has not considered are the laws that govern man. This is what the OT is trying to explain in stories.

The Science of Man, which are the five books of Moses, are laws that explain what your condition will be if you obey God's laws and what happens if you do not follow these laws. These laws are, in fact, truth, because they have been proven in the history of this world, and the history of the worlds that have preceded ours.

Natural law is truth when it can be proven and repeated. One truth is that feminism produces what looks like Sodom and Gomorrah. This is what feminism looks like in the end. Anything that changes God's natural order of things is Satanism. This is simply because of the binary world in which we live. You're either following your God which is law, or you're observing that which is in opposition to your God and law.

Man is matter and energy, and America has embraced feminism. The interactions of feminine energy have produced what the Bible warned it would produce.

Isaiah 3:12 (KJV) says,

> **As for my people, children are their oppressors, and women rule over them. O my people, they which lead thee cause thee to err, and destroy the way of thy paths.**

The destruction of God's people is a science. The condition of the world is a result of those who are Satanic and have manipulated every part of our Life. Do not make the error of thinking feminism is somehow about gender or the female.

Feminism is for men as well as women. Anyone who accepts this change in God's order has placed him or herself in opposition to God's Law.

> **And when the woman saw that the tree was good for food and that it was pleasant to the eyes, and a tree to be desired to make one wise, she took of the fruit thereof, and did eat, and gave also unto her husband with her; and he did eat. (Gen 3:6 KJV)**

It is not only important to understand your God but your enemy as well. Our story includes God, *his* story—history—removes God. The prophets of Satan have also spoken. What his-story reveals is that all races of people have to deal with the ungodly. This is why every race has dealt with slavery and oppression. What's more important than race is whom you follow or worship. Your beliefs are most important above all other things. This is why you are supposed to live not only among your own race but your own tribe within your race. People with the same set of beliefs are supposed to live among one another. Africans who sold Africans to Europeans have more in common with each other than Blacks or Whites who would never participate in those dealings. Those of the ungodly devalue life and have no respect for natural laws, natural laws being God's law. This would explain why some of the deadliest wars have been brother vs brother, Cain vs. Abel.

This is why every past civilization has had these biblical stories. It's a work of art and a testament to the intelligence of ancient people to put science into a story. Unfortunately, it's also very humbling. God's people are not supposed to endure these conditions.

My intention is not to add to or change the Word but to add understanding. In order to understand the Bible, you have to step outside of the Bible. The Bible is about the world, and the more we understand the world, the more we'll understand the Word. I never had any intentions of trying to sit down and understand the Bible. It was what I learned about the world which led me back to the Bible. In Chapter 2, we will continue with the duality that is at the heart of the Bible and the heart of creation.

Chapter 2

Duality is God's Creation and It is Very Consistent

The intent of the Bible is Life—maintaining Life and living as God intended. Any deviation from these laws will produce the negative outcomes that the Bible foretells. Contrary to what most may believe about the Bible, it's not a prophecy, it's a warning. **None of the evils that are foretold in the Bible have to happen.**

The science that is contained in the Bible is the same science used in computing. The world we live in is binary. In computing, this binary coding uses the 1 and 0 to represent off and on. This basic computing coding is used to represent what we see on our screens including colors, text, and graphics. This simple binary coding creates the complex levels of computing that we use today. This simple off and on of the 1 and 0 exist in the world we live in, and that binary coding of the world is Life and Death. **One (1) represents Life and zero (0) represents Death.** This coding exists in all of nature, from the macro to the micro.

The story of Adam and Eve introduces this binary with Genesis 2:9.

> **And out of the ground made the LORD God to grow every tree that is pleasant to the sight, and good for food; the tree of life also in the midst of the garden, and the tree of knowledge of good and evil. (Gen 2:9 KJV)**

The trees of life and of the knowledge of good and evil represent the choices of Life, one (1), and Death, zero (0). Once you begin to eat of the tree of knowledge of good and evil, you shall know Death. The question you may ask is, "why wouldn't God want Man to have knowledge?" The answer to that is, that **knowledge isn't truth**, and once it's presented, you won't know the difference. The one (1) and (0) in basic maths aren't equal, and neither are they equal in the binary world we live in.

The choices you make in life will either represent the 1 or the 0. The more zeros (0) the individual (or the society) makes, the closer he is to death. **This is why God's laws are to be maintained not only by the individual but by the family, the community, and the nation.** America's founders never intended America to be just a group of individuals, but societies within a nation. Of course, the individual is the most basic unit. Unlike the communists, I'm not saying to do away with the individual. That would be satanic and nonsensical.

Health and the Body

How does the one (1) and zero (0) look in health and maintaining one's body, something the Bible speaks about? Foods that contain the 1 are those foods that provide good health and maintain good health. These are your foods that grow and die. These foods are your leafy greens and vegetables—foods that when they are harvested for food can also be replanted and continue to grow. These are also fruits that have seeds. This is because they have Life. The poor health of most people can be directly attributed to their diet. Too many people eating too much-processed food is the cause of the health of so many failing. God's design for the body is complex, but its maintenance is very simple.

The ones (1) and zeros (0) of the body are pH, acidity, and alkalinity. The one (1) is alkalinity and the zero (0) is acidity. Processed food adds acidity to the body or zeros (0), resulting over time in poor health. To reverse the poor health of an individual, you simply need to begin to eliminate the zeros (0). Eliminate processed foods and those foods the Bible has stated as being unclean. Consistency in God's law is continued in that those creatures we are forbidden to eat consume death. This would explain why we are not to eat pork or shellfish. God's children are to choose "Life". Maintaining an alkaline body prevents sickness. We have lived in a godless environment for so long we have accepted poor health as normal and a natural process of aging, but it is not. The common cold should not be common. This is why we have dietary laws. Obedience to dietary law will maintain proper health.

We can continue this line of thought by observing how we farm and maintain our gardens. Leviticus 19:19 (KJV) says, "Ye shall keep my statutes. Thou shalt not let thy cattle gender with a diverse kind: thou shalt not sow thy field with mingled seed." There are plants that are edible and help to sustain life and there are weeds and plants that if not removed will kill the life-sustaining vegetation.

Although what I'm presenting is basic, my purpose is simply to illustrate the consistency in God's design. In agriculture to maintain a healthy garden or farm, you must rid your garden of anything that would destroy your vegetation or livestock. There are forces competing to destroy those things which give and maintain Life. It is the responsibility of God's people to maintain this balance. If Man fails at maintaining and separating from himself that which brings death, he'll reap what he sows. Whether that's poor health or a garden that doesn't produce.

Man and Beast

God's design for the world is complex but maintaining God's kingdom is simple.

Just like the previous examples, we have men and women who represent Life, one (1), and those who represent Death, zero (0). Those who represent Death are your Satanists or Luciferians. These men and women govern under communism and just like the devil they worship, their government goes by many names, Marxism, Leninism, Bolshevism, Leftism, Democratic Socialism, and more. These are the people the Bible is warning you about. This explains why the Bible instructs God's people to kill those who disobey his commandments. These men and women are the weeds among you.

> **[3] And hath gone and served other gods, and worshipped them,
> either the sun, or moon, or any of the host of heaven, which I
> have not commanded; [4] And it be told thee, and thou hast
> heard of it, and enquired diligently, and, behold, it be true,
> and the thing certain, that such abomination is wrought in
> Israel: [5] Then shalt thou bring forth that man or that woman,**

> **which have committed that wicked thing, unto thy gates, even that man or that woman, and shalt stone them with stones, till they die. [6] At the mouth of two witnesses, or three witnesses, shall he that is worthy of death be put to death; but at the mouth of one witness he shall not be put to death. [7] The hands of the witnesses shall be first upon him to put him to death, and afterward the hands of all the people. So thou shalt put the evil away from among you (Deuteronomy 17:3-7 KJV).**

The Bible begins by giving us the first tool we need in order to understand the rest of the Bible. That is *Duality,* which is defined by Merriam Webster as, a "dichotomy or a division into two especially mutually exclusive or contradictory groups or entities."

Duality: Heaven and earth, night and day, man and beast— The way God has created the world. God has created opposition to all things. All things God created, the duality of opposition, masculine and feminine, creates balance.

What the beast hates about us is that God's people can't be defeated unless the beast severs our relationship with God. We are to have a relationship with the Almighty. Once we allow the serpent to sever the relationship, he can destroy you. I will say more of the Beast in chapter 3.

This duality transcends all things the Creator has made. It's God's way of maintaining balance or equilibrium. All things have an opposing force, and as we begin reading Genesis this truth becomes evident as outlined in the following passages. You will see that, essentially, we live in a binary world.

> **In the beginning, God created the heavens and the earth (Gen 1:1 KJV).**
>
> **And God saw the light, that it was good: and God divided the light from the darkness (Gen 1:4 KJV).**
>
> **And God made two great lights; the greater light to rule the day, and the lesser light to rule the night: he made the stars also (Gen 1:16 KJV).**
>
> **[24] And God said, Let the earth bring forth the living creature after his kind, cattle, and creeping thing, and beast of the earth after his kind: and it was so. [25] And God made the beast of the earth after his kind, and cattle after their kind, and every thing that creepeth upon the earth after his kind: and God saw that it was good (Gen 1:24-25 KJV).**
>
> **So God created man in his own image, in the image of God created he him; male and female created he them (Gen 1:27 KJV).**

So in the beginning we have our first list of dualities, light-dark, heaven-earth, male-female, man-beast. This concept of duality is important for understanding the world around us. In understanding the WORD, it is also important to understand the WORLD. Grasping how God's design looks and works will help us to understand the Bible. Grasping the Bible will help us to understand the world.

Genesis details the Creation of the world. This creation is binary, where all things HE has created are male and female, and all things he has created have an opposition: night and day, life and death, man and beast. Every creature has an opposition: Cat vs. Mouse, Dog vs. Cat, Lion vs. Hyena, etc. This opposition creates balance on Earth. Man's opposition is the beast. Beast, according to the Bible, is a type of Man who lives among us. These beasts the Bible speaks of are those who I refer to in later chapters as Satanist/Godless.

Male and Female

The Creator has given us another clue about his design by telling us that 'He' is male and female and that we were designed in that image.

> **So God created man in his own image, in the image of God created he him; male and female created he them (Gen 1:27 KJV).**

This duality is important because in order to create you must have the masculine as well as the feminine. The implications of this are that some things that we have come to accept as properly labeled are not. For instance, most people say that the realms of the mind are the conscious and the subconscious. The conscious mind is where the discernible thoughts are, the thoughts you are having and you know you are having them. The subconscious mind is where those vague thoughts are that you may not know you are having. They quietly affect your emotional state. They cause you to do things and you don't know why you're doing it. The reason is there in the subconscious mind, but you don't discern it without bringing it to awareness in the conscious mind.

However, this is wrong. Your mind is not conscious-subconscious, but rather masculine-feminine. It is the properties of both the masculine mind and the feminine mind that give birth to new thoughts. Your car battery doesn't have positive and negative terminals but male and female terminals. Male and female are determined by the flow of energy from the masculine to the feminine. This transfer of energy from masculine to feminine creates energy. The Sun and Moon are also masculine and feminine. God's design is so consistent that the cyle of the moon and the average cycle for women is 28 days.

The dualities that exist in God's design are also found in the Bible. The Bible is both Masculine-Militant and Feminine-Spiritual, a topic we will touch on later. As we continue reading the Bible, we see that man is confronted with this duality.

> **And out of the ground made the LORD God to grow every tree that is pleasant to the sight, and good for food; the tree of life also in the midst of the garden, and the tree of knowledge of good and evil (Gen 2:9 KJV).**

The Tree of Life is represented by God, and the tree of good and evil is that which is in opposition to God. God representing life is explained in Genesis 2:7 (KJV). "And the LORD God formed man of the dust of the ground and breathed into his nostrils the breath of life, and man became a living soul."

The Tree of Death

The trees in the midst of the garden could have been simply named the Tree of Life and the Tree of Death, but as we continue dissecting the Bible, we can understand why the Tree of Knowledge is used instead of "Death." Every child born will be given the Tree of Life or the Tree of Good and Evil. *This will inevitably be determined by the decisions of the mother and the father.* When the option to choose the Tree of Good and Evil is presented, it is represented as *knowledge*, whereas if given an option of death over life it would be too easy an option to decline.

The Design

The structure of the Bible contains the duality that is described on the first page of the OT. That duality consists of the Book of Life (OT) and the Book of Death (NT), the Book of Law (OT) and the Book of Love (NT), Rulers (OT) and Slaves (NT), Adam (OT) and Eve (NT), Masculine (OT) and Feminine (NT).

The duality that God speaks of on the first pages is also displayed in how he designed the animal world. While some creatures behave more decently, there are those whose behavior is absolutely beastlike. There are creatures that have social structure and order, while there are those, like the hyena, that will eat their young. The female hyena has a penis like the male hyena's and has a matriarchal order. The hyena is truly a beast after its kind. The hyena male is weaker and smaller than the female and lives a shorter life. This is due to the males eating last and having a poorer diet. This is also what happens to Man if he allows the structure of his family to change. A matriarchal family structure produces weaker men.

A matriarchal family is one that has accepted feminism. Under feminine leadership, it will produce, more often than not, both men and women who display feminine characteristics. The most extreme characteristics are homosexuality and homicide. The least extreme feminine behavior of the male is his inability to lead, the ability to provide for and protect his children. This is also the behavior of the male hyena, it is the bitch (female hyena) that fights the lion. The feminine characteristics of wild beasts like the hyena will become the behavior of Men. The

Hyena also kills without discretion and its invitation for an attack is weakness, unlike the Lion, who kills to provide and protect. The feminized Man and the Woman, like the hyena, will fight for the right to destroy their young.

The destruction of God's people is a science. Everything the OT is telling you not to do, the enemy of God's people will tell you it's ok. Today the feminist Man and Woman do not fear God and their godless behavior is on display.

> [16] **And he said, When ye do the office of a midwife to the Hebrew women, and see them upon the stools; if it be a son, then ye shall kill him: but if it be a daughter, then she shall live.** [17] **But the midwives feared God, and did not as the king of Egypt commanded them, but saved the men children alive. (Exodus 1:16-17 KJV)**

Again, contrast that with the structure and order of the patriarchal lion. The lion has the sole responsibility of making sure all the lionesses and cubs are protected and provided for. Today it's the Hyena who has convinced the Lioness she doesn't need a Lion and that it's okay to kill her unborn. If the Hyena could speak this would be what she would communicate to the Lioness and that would be a victory for the Hyena. Without the protection of the Lion and a shrinking number of Lion cubs, the Hyenas would be free to rule the plains. The Hyenas, Men, and Women, of the world, like the Lion, would have their *Pride.* America has accepted the culture of feminism and we behave like Hyenas.

What you'll also notice is that all creatures obey God's dietary law. Those creatures that live the longest, turtles, those that grow the largest, Elephants, and those that are the strongest, gorillas, only eat vegetation. The Bible is also in alignment with these teachings of only eating certain foods or clean beasts.

What about those creatures that are "after their kind?" They eat all things, like the pig who will literally eat anything that is placed in front of it, including feces and other dead pigs.

Man has free-will to disobey God's dietary law, and disobedience to God's dietary law leads to poor health. All things God has created have laws. The Beast, however, and those things created after his kind, are not required to follow God's law. God's protections are for his followers, those who choose to follow after the Beast relinquish that protection.

I've been asked if God forgives. I believe the Creator can do all things. If he chooses to forgive, then it's done. The problem however is that the world he has created for us is unforgiving. If I tell my child not to go near the fire and he does, I can forgive him for disobeying, but that is not going to keep the fire from burning him.

There is order to the way God created the world. God's children keep the laws of his order, and those who are not God's children do not. We will discuss this further in the next chapter.

Chapter 3

All People Are God's Creation, but Not All People are God's Children

To determine whether your god is the true God, look at the laws that your god gives you. You should be able to reconcile the laws given to Man with the design of the world. The laws that God gives are so that those created in his image will not fall prey or become enslaved. When we look at the design of the world we'll see that God has created many types of species and within those species many subspecies. One thing noticeable is that species typically don't interbreed in nature, which shows obedience to God's design and to God's Law. Deuteronomy 7:3 says, "Neither shalt thou make marriages with them; thy daughter thou shalt not give unto his son, nor his daughter shalt thou take unto thy son" (KJV).

We have seen what happens with horses and donkeys when they are unnaturally forced to mate, which produces mules who are not capable of reproduction. What might be implied may seem disturbing for some to grasp, but we must follow the truth wherever it takes us. We have been told that we are all God's children, but the truth is that it isn't so. What is true is that we are all God's creation, but we are not all created in his image. 1 Samuel 2:12 says, "Now the sons of Eli were sons of Belial; they knew not the LORD" (KJV).

We look at the world and see that God has created various species and subspecies, but somehow we can't believe that there is more than one type of man. One thing that is certain is that God's design is consistent. Often the truth hides in plain sight. You can't simply look at a person's physical appearance and determine if that person is truly of God. You must observe the Laws they maintain and whether they are consistent with the nature of God. How does the image of God on earth look? It would appear as man and woman being as one, which is how we were designed. It would appear orderly, structured, and clean. The men would know who their enemy is, and the women would also be keepers of God's law. The laws of the men of God are of a higher order than man's law. He who was not created in God's image seeks to supplant God and have God's children worship him and obey his laws.

Most of us were taught to have a love for all the people of the world.

This will be difficult for most to handle because of how we were taught to understand the world and the people in it. God has created different types of animals and within that animal family, many groups. This design is also consistent with man. We have different families of Man, and within these families of men exist different kinds of men.

The truth is that God's design is consistent. He has created different sorts of animals of the same kind, and he has done the same regarding man. All men are not of the same kind. Broadly, there are the people of God and men that are of the Beast.

Most have traditionally accepted the idea of all people being one human race and all children of God. Yet, if that is true how can anyone explain the evils that some men do? How can anyone explain men of God killing children, raping women, eating corpses, sleeping with corpses, pedophilia, and murder? Are these simply men of God behaving badly? The answer to that is absolutely not. We're all God's creation but we're not all God's children.

All men are not created equal. To be sure, they are created equal in the sense that Jefferson meant. All should have inalienable rights, but not all men are the same, *and not all disobedience is the same.* I am speaking of some dark things. In the Christian faith (NT), a key doctrine is the doctrine of total depravity. The foundation of what is known as the gospel message is that, according to Paul,

> 9 **...all, both Jews and Greeks, are under sin,**
>
> 10 **as it is written: "None is righteous, no, not one;**
>
> 11 **no one understands; no one seeks for God.**
>
> 12 **All have turned aside; together they have become worthless; no one does good, not even one."**
>
> 13 **"Their throat is an open grave; they use their tongues to deceive." "The venom of asps is under their lips."**

14 "Their mouth is full of curses and bitterness."

15 "Their feet are swift to shed blood;

16 in their paths are ruin and misery,

17 and the way of peace they have not known."

18 "There is no fear of God before their eyes." (Ro 3:9b-18 ESV)

And, 23 "...all have sinned and fall short of the glory of God, 24 and are justified by his grace as a gift, through the redemption that is in Christ Jesus (Ro 3:23b-24 ESV).

Christians are taught that everyone is evil. To be sure, everyone sins sometimes—a white lie here and a bit of gluttony there, but no, everyone is not the same. Though we may all "fall short" of perfection, do not avert your gaze from pure evil where it exists. Ask yourself: Would you worship Satan, raping and impregnating 11-year-olds, only to cut the baby out prematurely so you can eat it in your rituals? Because there are those who do that?

Would you enslave people, murder, rob, or commit all manner of sexual crimes? There is a species of human who does this routinely whenever they can get away with it. We are not all the same. There is a fundamental difference in kind. There are men among us whose nature is godless. They're natural killers. The nature of the Beast is to be true to his design. No amount of love will change the blood that flows within the Beast.

1 John 3:12 KJV says, "Not as Cain, who was of that wicked one, and slew his brother. And wherefore slew he him? Because his own works were evil, and his brother's righteous" (KJV).

These men are the weeds among God's children. This is why God separated the light from the dark. This is why there's division among those things that God has created. In a world where evil has flourished, it suggests that men of God have gone against the natural order God has created. We have eaten from the tree of knowledge and now we know death.

The question for some may be, why would God create a world with men who are evil? Or why would we have things in this world that we're not supposed to have? The answer is free-will. God has given you the choice to live as you choose. You can live the way God intended or you can suffer through a life that's in opposition to God.

Genesis 1:28 says,

> **And God blessed them, and God said unto them, Be fruitful, and multiply, and replenish the earth, and subdue it: and have dominion over the fish of the sea, and over the fowl of the air, and over every living thing that moveth upon the earth (KJV).**

Job 12:7-8 says,

> [7] **But ask now the beasts, and they shall teach thee; and the fowls of the air, and they shall tell thee:** [8] **Or speak to the earth, and it shall teach thee: and the fishes of the sea shall declare unto thee. (KJV)**

Men have an enemy, beasts. But the Bible talks about the Beasts — men who look like you and me but are not. They control the world. We're all God's creation, but we're not all his children. Those who are not his children do not have to follow the laws in the Bible. There is a divine bloodline and a demonic bloodline. The lines aren't drawn according to race. Every race has godless among them and it's up to all people to find them.

Adam and Eve

In the third chapter of the Bible, we see the tragedy of the fall of Adam. They had been given the ultimate choice that all of the children of God are given: Life or Death. That is, don't eat the fruit of the Tree of Knowledge and live, or eat of it and die. A man comes along, the Serpent, the true Beast, Satan, who tempts the woman to rebel against the law of God. This passage is mysterious because it is so brief. But what must be understood is that much more went on in the exchange between Eve and the Serpent. Why does 1 John 3:12 say, "Not as Cain, who was of that wicked one" (KJV)?

Beasts

What follows may be the most difficult to accept or believe. If you are of the mindset that God is capable of all things. Then this falls into that category of things that are the most unbelievable. There are "people" who live among us who are not human. The Bible refers to these beings as "beasts" and that's an accurate and literal description.

The false idea of aliens is given by the enemy so that you may look up when you actually should look down. The natural habitat of the beast is below. Which means hell is local. These are the beings past civilizations were warning us about. These are the beast the Bible is warning us about. The nature of the beast is in opposition to man, it's in opposition to God's people. This is the curse of the fallen angels and men who are in opposition to God's children. **If these beasts, who are now in**

control of governments, had the ability to leave Earth and escape God's punishment, they would.

Who does the Bible say that they are?

Genesis 1:24-25 says,

> **[24] And God said, Let the earth bring forth the living creature after his kind, cattle, and creeping thing, and beast of the earth after his kind: and it was so. [25] And God made the beast of the earth after his kind, and cattle after their kind, and every thing that creepeth upon the earth after his kind: and God saw that it was good. (KJV)**

In certain epochs of earth's history, the Beasts were easily distinguishable. We are in a period of time in man's cycle or his season when one can't distinguish who is Man and who is beast simply by looking at them. The above Bible verse is trying to convey that there are creatures that God has created that are in the image of their kind. Just as there are creatures that are created in the image of his kind. So in this season of man. **The only way to truly know who is of God and who isn't is by observing the behavior of those around you.**

What are the behaviors of the beast? Any of the behaviors that you see in the animal world about unclean beasts, those who are created after 'their' kind, these men will have those same behaviors. **These men, these beasts, will have all the behaviors you see in dogs, pigs, bats, and rats.** These men will have an attraction and sex with those around them with total disregard for relationships, and there will be incest. They will be as comfortable in filth as God's people are in cleanliness. What some would refer to as fetishes, these men take pleasure in obscenities. They will enjoy consumption or pleasure with bile like a dog. They'll love the drinking of blood like mosquitoes and bats and also cannibalism. The elevating of the feminine over the masculine, like the hyena, will be a feature.

Feminism, as discussed previously, is accepting satanism. It breaks down the social order. Feminism isn't strictly for women, it's for everyone, and if accepted, produces what it was intended to produce family breakdown and homosexuality. Homosexuality doesn't produce life.

These beasts also believe it's okay to sacrifice or abort children. And all of these acts that are common in nature of animals eating their offspring, these beasts have also done. Some are born beasts and some choose them.

As the beast moves God's children away from the law, the children of God will also begin to take pleasure in these obscenities and they also will know death.

Some Born Beasts, Some Choose them

Some of us are born predisposed to these behaviors, and some of us choose to align ourselves with those who are cursed. This is the free-will God has given us. The animals he created cannot choose, but you can. If you choose poorly, you will suffer as the beast. The OT is founded on truth and absolutes. This is just one of many.

Your genetics don't only affect how you look, they predispose you to certain behaviors. It has to do with the blood that flows through your veins. This is why you are also not to allow your children to procreate with them. This would also explain why there are customs among some groups that require arranged marriages. Past generations understood the importance of not mixing the blood of different people. Of course, as time passes, children will challenge customs and traditions, because they simply do not understand why.

There are also those who are allergic to the sun and must live a nocturnal life.

God said the punishment for the Serpent would be for him to go upon his belly, which means he will go into the belly of the earth, Gen 3:14. The world goes through seasons or cycles that last 1000's years. We as God's people are currently in the winter of this cycle. When the earth moves toward summer, the Beast becomes afflicted. He cannot tolerate the sun, because he's meant for the belly of the earth. Black or white, the sun will literally boil their skin. Have you ever heard of Porphyria? We have people already there. The beasts must feed on the blood of God's people, the blood of man. They must ingest it. These are the people who rule the world. They know who they are. We assume they're like us, God's children. They know everyone is not like them. The duality of what is required of Man and what is required of the beast is explained in Genesis.

Genesis 9:5 KJV

> **And surely your blood of your lives will I require; at the hand of every beast will I require it, and at the hand of man; at the hand of every man's brother will I require the life of man.**

In the NT it says there will be a 1000-year reign of Christ, the Millennium. Satan will be let out at the end of it to raise havoc, but ultimately be defeated. We're moving toward this end. Why does the Beast have to be so evil? It is because he was designed to be. His survival requires our destruction. He wants us to suffer as he suffers, especially God's people.

This is the punishment of God that is built into the design. There are men of God who must follow the law, 'His' children, and there are beasts whose survival requires their destruction. Victory for God's people does not require us to behave like the beast and set out on a mission of destruction to start a war. Children of God defeat the Beast by bringing Life to the World and maintaining law and order. I've heard all my life that Blacks have a racial problem, but they do not. They have a ratio problem. The ratio of the beast among us is exceeding the number of Godly.

Again, nature demonstrates this with the Lions. There is always a threat of attack from the Hyena, yet as long as there remains the structure of order, headed by a male Lion. The Hyena against its nature to kill and destroy the Lion keeps its distance. Even when the male Lion is outnumbered by the Hyena, we get a visual depiction of God's truth and God's covenant with his children…

Leviticus 26:8-9 KJV

> **And five of you shall chase an hundred, and an hundred of you shall put ten thousand to flight: and your enemies shall fall before you by the sword. [9] For I will have respect unto you, and make you fruitful, and multiply you, and establish my covenant with you.**

Here is an example of "Beastly" evil: People in Papua New Guinea develop Prion disease. This blood disorder attacks brain function and eventually kills. This group practices funerary cannibalism, and some people even exist by feeding off men and women. All around the globe cave art shows evidence of cannibalism. This is a grievous evil.

During the 1920s Russian famine, peasants were forced into cannibalism. This was done in Russia to other Russians. This should help to explain why we currently have a war between Russia and Ukraine, two countries who were at one time united as one under the U.S.S.R. Ukraine is the region of Russia where millions starved under the communist leadership of Stalin, from 1929 into the early 1930s. This is the evil perpetrated by Satanists against any people regardless of race. Russians were starved to the point where they began to practice cannibalism, eating their children.

During this Russian famine, we get a sense of the type of humanity Satanists/communists have for human suffering.

> *Trotsky to the dying Ukrainian peasants - "You are starving? - This is not famine yet... When your women start eating their children then you may come and say, "we are starving".*
>
> **–Leon Trotsky**

These are the stories from history that help to answer my question. "Why do Whites hate Blacks?'

I can now see my ignorance in asking this question because it is not Whites who hate Blacks it has nothing to do with race. I like many others was taught to see the world thru the lens of race, instead of the eyes God gave us. I understand now that we're hated because of our God. We're hated because if we do as he has instructed then it will mean defeat for the Satanist.

Race has been used as a tool to keep God's people fighting among one another instead of dealing with our common enemy.

Let's not forget that today in America, communist Russia, and China owns American food production and farmland. This has been allowed under the leadership of Democrats and Republicans. What do you think is going to happen next?

This chapter is focused on cannibalism but I also wanted to note that the communist Red Army allowed and encouraged the rape of women and children during WWII. What's also being reported is that these atrocities are happening again in the current war between Ukraine and Russia, as women, young boys, and girls have been reported as being raped.

I mention this because the devil in Europe is no different than the devil in Africa.

Gibril Massaquoi, nicknamed 'Angel Gabriel', –the Angel of Death– is to stand trial for war crimes. Massaquoi a commander of the Sierra Leone rebel group, the Revolutionary United Front stands accused of mass rape, mutilation -hacking off limbs-, cutting up his victims, and eating them.

Massaquoi is also accused of forcing civilians to include children into buildings and torching them, drugging children, and creating armies of child soldiers. These rebel forces killed an estimated 250,000 and this does not include the numbers of those raped and mutilated.

These child soldiers were forced to participate in rituals of cannibalism because the leadership believed it would give them physical and spiritual power.

Europeans practiced cannibalism for medicinal reasons in the 16th and 17th centuries. Consuming the powdered remains of the dead and drinking blood. They preferred the warm blood of those who had recently died or were executed. There was still yet another preference for the blood of young men and virgin women.

> *"We preserve our life with the death of others. In a dead thing, insensate life remains which, when it is reunited with the stomachs of the living, regains sensitive and intellectual life."*
>
> **-Leonardo da Vinci**

Ancient Roman soldiers consumed the blood of their fallen enemies hoping to gain vitality. And all throughout history, there are accounts of this. In caves throughout the world, bones indicate the practice of cannibalism and the use of children's skulls as cups and adult skulls as bowls.

Again, are these just misguided men of God behaving badly? These are examples of the evil that is in the world because the Creator's children have stood by and allowed the weeds to grow uninterrupted among us. The Bible warned us of these things, disobedience to God results in death and slavery.

Leviticus 26:16 KJV

> **I also will do this unto you; I will even appoint over you terror, consumption, and the burning ague, that shall consume the eyes, and cause sorrow of heart: and ye shall sow your seed in vain, for your enemies shall eat it.**

The darkness of communism had manifested as it always will, but more on that in chapter 9 when we discuss the political implications of this war.

The Dead Sea scrolls, discovered in 1947 in a cave near Qumran, describe the war between the sons of light and sons of darkness. In the Book of the Dead of the Egyptians, we see the same. We've done this all before, we've failed before, and we've failed again because we've let the world come under the control of the Satanic. God has created the world in a dualistic way because that is how it has to be. To have light, there must be darkness. To have good, there must be evil. For good to win, evil must be vanquished. God has created and called his children to follow him and to win the world for the light. But we fail, again and again, allowing evil to take more and more ground in each cycle. In the end, if we don't wake up and honor what God has called us to do, only an intervention from God will break the power of Satan. Has this happened before? Of course. Remember Noah's flood? Once God looks on the earth and sees that "the wickedness of man [is] great in the earth, and that every imagination of the thoughts of his heart [is] only evil continually" (Gen 6:5 KJV), he will come and start over.

Revelation 16:8-9 says,

> **8 And the fourth angel poured out his vial upon the sun; and power was given unto him to scorch men with fire.**
>
> **9 And men were scorched with great heat, and blasphemed the name of God, which hath power over these plagues: and they repented not to give him glory.**

One way to recognize those who represent Death is that their lifestyles and the lifestyles they promote, do not produce Life. Legalized abortion is an idea of the Satanists and through indoctrination, they have convinced some women that the destruction of their children brings back their freedoms. This is what happens when the binary of Life and Death attempts to coexist. They can't. One must annihilate the other. This is done by confusion. Where there is confusion, there is the devil and his Tree of Knowledge.

1 John 3:12 says,

> **Not as Cain, who was of that wicked one, and slew his brother. And wherefore slew he him? Because his own works were evil, and his brother's righteous. (KJV)**

In today's world, all people are being sold on the idea of interracial relationships and total disobedience to the law. Not only should different races not mix, but those who worship different gods also shouldn't lay with one another either. It's not about race, it's about blood. All races of people have these beasts among them with which they must deal effectively. Man is supposed to separate themselves first by race, then by tribe. Your tribe is made up of those who worship as you worship and live as you live.

Different tribes, and different people, can be allies of one another, for and against those who represent the beast. This is currently the mistake God's people are making. We've allowed the enemy to divide God's people because we no longer know the difference.

Leviticus 20:15-16 says,

> **[15] And if a man lie with a beast, he shall surely be put to death:
> and ye shall slay the beast. [16] And if a woman approach unto
> any beast, and lie down thereto, thou shalt kill the woman, and the beast: they shall surely be put to death; their blood shall be upon them.**

Blacks and Whites in America are making the same mistake. We are aligning ourselves with those who look like us but they're not us. The beast uses loyal Whites and Blacks and those all over the planet to create the condition the world is currently in. The history of man is cyclical, and as we progress through these seasons we have different challenges. This season began with the birth of Jesus, in 0 AD. *Anno Domini* is a Latin phrase meaning the "year of our Lord."

Luke 23:44-45 says,

> **[44] And it was about the sixth hour, and there was a darkness
> over all the earth until the ninth hour. [45] And the sun was
> darkened, and the veil of the temple was rent in the midst. (KJV)**

Matthew 27:50-54 says,

> **[50] Jesus, when he had cried again with a loud voice, yielded up
> the ghost. [51] And, behold, the veil of the temple was rent in
> twain from the top to the bottom; and the earth did quake,
> and the rocks rent; [52] And the graves were opened; and many
> bodies of the saints which slept arose, [53] And came out of the
> graves after his resurrection, and went into the holy city, and
> appeared unto many. [54] Now when the centurion, and they**

> **that were with him, watching Jesus, saw the earthquake, and those things that were done, they feared greatly, saying, Truly this was the Son of God. (KJV)**

These seasons of Man last thousands of years and these changes of seasons appear to be marked by heavenly events in the sky and earthquakes.

Genesis 1:14 says,

> **And God said, Let there be lights in the firmament of the heaven to divide the day from the night; and let them be for signs, and for seasons, and for days, and years. (KJV)**

Why is it important to understand the seasons of Man? As we approach our next season it will become clear who is Man and who is beast. This is a concern for the beast because it will become clear what God's people need to do. If any of this sounds like a horror story, it is. Monsters are real, and for a season they appear like men. The curse of the beast is that he must return to the caves from which he came because history is not linear but cyclical like seasons. Contrary to what we've been taught, it's the modern man that goes into caves and devolves into his true self, which is a beast.

Earlier, I mentioned that those creatures created like 'their' kind will display all of the behaviors that you see in the animal world of the unclean beasts. This is true. One behavior I didn't include is that of the pig when separated from captivity. The pig depending on what side of the fence it's on will appear differently. A captive pig can be handled, whereas a wild pig or boar is deadly. These men, like the beast that are created after 'their' kind become feral, live in caves only coming out to feed under the cover of darkness.

On the day of judgment, which is the beginning of the next season, the beast will become like wild boar, deadly. The underworld is the natural habitat and curse of the beast. If you choose to follow the beast, on the Day of Judgment you will also suffer his fate, which is why you are not supposed to let the beast have access to your blood.

Genesis 3:14 says,

> **And the Lord God said unto the serpent, Because thou hast done this, thou art cursed above all cattle, and above every beast of the field; upon thy belly shalt thou go, and dust shalt thou eat all the days of thy life. (KJV)**

The curse as outlined here in this verse in Genesis is that the serpent goes upon his belly. That belly the verse is speaking of, is in the Earth. This truth is continued in the NT and the answer to the parable that is suggested by Jesus in the NT. Matthew 13:36-43 says,

> **36 Then Jesus sent the multitude away, and went into the house:**
> **and his disciples came unto him, saying, Declare unto us the**
> **parable of the tares of the field. 37 He answered and said unto**
> **them, He that soweth the good seed is the Son of man; 38 The**
> **field is the world; the good seed are the children of the**
> **kingdom; but the tares are the children of the wicked one; 39**
> **The enemy that sowed them is the devil; the harvest is the end**
> **of the world; and the reapers are the angels. 40 As therefore the**
> **tares are gathered and burned in the fire; so shall it be in the**
> **end of this world. 41 The Son of man shall send forth his angels,**

> **and they shall gather out of his kingdom all things that offend,
> and them which do iniquity; 42 And shall cast them into a
> furnace of fire: there shall be wailing and gnashing of teeth. 43
> Then shall the righteous shine forth as the sun in the kingdom
> of their Father. Who hath ears to hear, let him hear. (KJV)**

The only thing that will satisfy his hunger is the blood of man and his flesh. The beast will satisfy his hunger by breaking the bones of man and eating his marrow like the flesh of crab legs.

1 Corinthians 15:51-52

> **51 Behold, I shew you a mystery; We shall not all sleep, but we
> shall all be changed, 52 In a moment, in the twinkling of an eye,
> at the last trump: for the trumpet shall sound, and the dead
> shall be raised incorruptible, and we shall be changed. (KJV)**

> **8 And the fourth angel poured out his vial upon the sun; and
> power was given unto him to scorch men with fire. 9 And men
> were scorched with great heat, and blasphemed the name of
> God, which hath power over these plagues: and they repented
> not to give him glory. (Rev 16:8-9)**

As we move into the next season of man, the increased radiation of the sun will force those who are in opposition to the S.U.N of God to seek refuge in the Earth, only coming out to feed under the cover of darkness, like other nocturnal beasts. This is not about the protection that melanin gives you from sunburn, but the blood. The Black Men and Women of the Earth are just as susceptible to suffering from the return of the S.U.N. of God as anyone else. If you have not protected your blood and have allowed access to your blood through drug use, syringes, and promiscuous sex, then you may very well suffer the same fate as the beast. The beast understands his curse and wants nothing more than the children of God to suffer as he will suffer.

In 1859, we received a warning shot. The Carrington Event. This will happen again, but this time it will not be for just a couple of days. The cycle is coming to a completion.

Revelation 20:1-3 says,

> **[1] And I saw an angel come down from heaven, having the key of the bottomless pit and a great chain in his hand. [2] And he laid hold on the dragon, that old serpent, which is the Devil, and Satan, and bound him a thousand years, 3 And cast him into the bottomless pit, and shut him up, and set a seal upon him, that he should deceive the nations no more, till the thousand years should be fulfilled: and after that he must be loosed a little season. (KJV)**

This is already beginning to happen to those who have Porphyria. God is judging the world. The only thing that can stay his hand is if we, his children, will judge it and bring order by obeying his laws. Today, because of modern medical advances, people are somewhat able to cope with these conditions. There are men who receive blood transfusions once a week, in order to deal with these disorders. What happens when the power goes out (and it will)? It's not the return of the SON, it's the return of the S-U-N. These solar events are called CME, coronal mass ejections, and they will get worse.

The Sun has its seasons, there are periods where the Sun's radiation is higher and when it's at or is reaching its peak, the time is nearing for the beast to return to his hell. It is during this time when the beast will deceive all men to accept the mark so that they may also, suffer his fate.

What the world shows us is that Man's history isn't linear it's cyclical, and seasonal. These seasons last millenniums. Once the beast and those who follow the beast are sealed in the belly of the earth only coming out at night to feed. The children of God have an opportunity to re-establish God's kingdom on earth. God will once again dwell among us and we are now tasked with maintaining HIS law and warning future generations of what's to come. Modern Men will return to the caves and when his seal is removed as the Sun's seasons change the beast will once again emerge.

The Sun approaching its peak will begin to change men and we will have a separating of the wheat from the tares. The tares will be burned by the sun, but the wheat will have God's protection.

The Sun will return man to darkness. All electrical systems will fail, many electrical devices and items attached to them will burn and men and women will in an instant be returned to how God created them.

Evidence of what lies ahead happened on September 01, 1859, when we had a Carrington event. This event is named after the man who first recorded a CME, coronal mass ejection. This CME burned the only existing electrical components at that time which were the telegraph machines. The electrical lines and items surrounding the machines burned. While the electrical systems that connected these machines may have burned and become disabled, it is also recorded that there was enough ambient electricity in the atmosphere to allow telegraph machines to continue to send and receive messages. Also during this event night, skies became day, and auroras which are normally only seen in the polar regions were visible across the planet.

In May 1921, we have the New York Railroad Storm which started fires worldwide. This CME also created auroras that could be seen in many parts of the world which normally don't have auroras and again the destruction wasn't very severe because the world wasn't as connected as it is today.

We have another incident, more recent, which happened on March 13, 1989. This solar storm took out the electrical grid that supplied parts of Canada and the northeast United States. The blackouts led to looting in the night streets of NY and things hadn't returned to normal until the power was restored. Also, during this event, you had a visible aurora that appeared further south than normal.

These events can be considered warning shots for what will eventually become the final blow that will reset man. God did not create us to live in opposition to his design or among the Godless.

Evidence of this can be found all over the world. There are caves in America such as the one in Sweetwater, TN which is home to the largest underground lake in North America, and caves in Missouri where truckers currently and routinely make deliveries. There are literally caves in just about every state in the union.

What about the thousand miles of caverns that stretch across Europe? Turkey is currently home to the largest underground city to be discovered with an estimated capacity to hold over 50,000 people. Guyaju Caves in China cover 24 acres.

Some of these caves are naturally made, others were made by previous civilizations thousands of years ago. Modern scientists want us to believe that a prehistoric man carved thousands of miles of caves using a hammer and chisel. No, they did what modern man is doing today which are major digs around the world, in preparation for their return to the belly of the Earth. Large living spaces have already been created and continue to be developed around the world. Remember it's the modern man who returns to the caves and what emerges is a feral man, a beast.

Isaiah 2:19-21 KJV

> **And they shall go into the holes of the rocks, and into the caves of the earth, for fear of the LORD, and for the glory of his majesty, when he ariseth to shake terribly the earth. [20] In that day a man shall cast his idols of silver, and his idols of gold, which they made each one for himself to worship, to the moles and to the bats; [21] To go into the clefts of the rocks, and into the tops of the ragged rocks, for fear of the LORD, and for the glory of his majesty, when he ariseth to shake terribly the earth.**

Recently in 2016 the Gotthard tunnel was completed stretching 35 miles through the Alps in Switzerland. One section of tunnel 7 miles long under the North Atlantic Ocean in the Faroe Islands was completed in 2020 and many underground and underwater highways are being created under the guise of mass transit all over the world. This is deception because the world population has collapsed and there isn't any need for large-scale highway construction. Actually in some parts of the world, including some large American cities, they are demolishing above-ground interstates in an attempt to further hide depopulation.

The behavior of the enemy of God's people should further be an indication that the Satanists believe your God will do what he said he would.

A Relationship with God

God spoke to Moses and said, I am that, I am. Then the truth, is that it is. Knowing the truth is not a religion. God does not care about your religion or what you may believe. He wants us to establish a relationship with 'Him'. Our Creator and the truth that's outlined in his design existed before we were formed and this truth will exist after we are gone. It is our responsibility to give our children the truth so that we may continue our relationship with the Almighty and that we may enjoy the world the way he intended.

For some, this will be the greatest time to be alive and for others, this will be the worst time to be alive. Some of us alive today will see the truth of God unfold. Now is the time to find your way back to your Heavenly Father and re-establish your relationship with the Creator.

Part Two

Application

Chapter 4

Race, Segregation, and Slavery

Disintegration

What blacks were sold was integration. What we received is *dis*integration. The happy communities we had no longer exist. The place where elders were respected and children were safe, where fathers stayed married to mothers and raised their children, disappeared overnight. The world as I experienced it would not be known by my children. If you watch the evening news, you will see the hostile world as it is now. The killings, the so-called black-on-black crime. This is not the world I grew up in, but it is the world we've created.

Growing up, everything I needed in life was within walking distance from my home. I could go to the library or the movie theater without ever crossing the street. I walked to school and I walked back home again, though I was young. We were taught as children to be independent. We understood that we were learning to steward our own lives so that one day we could steward a family and a community.

Today, after sixty years of welfare and integration, black leaders are calling for "their people" to spend their money at each other's "black-owned businesses." This strikes my ears as ridiculous coming from them because before we were supposedly liberated by forced integration, that's exactly what we did. The movie theater I walked to was black owned and so were many of the stores in my community. No campaign or slogan was required for us to support black-owned businesses. It was our life.

Yet, Integration Was a "Success"

As I look back on those years in school with the benefit of age and wisdom, I can say that integration was a huge "success", if success means accomplishing what you set out to accomplish by an endeavor. For those who wanted integration and those who enacted it, it is still a success today, though they will tell you there "is still so much to be done."

Integration coupled with the creation of the welfare state has brought the black race to a spiritually impoverished place and has actually not helped whites either. This is a difficult topic to discuss because there was some good intention in *some* people when it came to both of these atrocities. Even today, it would be hard for a white person to accept that integration was a bad thing. They've been sold on the idea that they, every single one of them, are responsible for slavery, Jim Crow, the KKK, and anything crime or oppression ever perpetrated against a black person. Whites were told that it was unfair that there was a disparity between the average black person and the average white person. But now, because of these so-called solutions, the disparity is greater than it ever was. Add to that fact that the ultimate reason for integration and the welfare state was a demonic breakdown of human society and a violation of God's biblical principles of separation and purity, and you can see how we've already lost.

Each One is An Individual

These kinds of things, along with the killing of black men, make the idea of racism an easy sell to blacks. But even after all those years of racism, discrimination, and oppression suffered by blacks, I have always maintained an ability to judge each person as an individual. I've never let the world change who I am, nor given other people the power to cause me to hate. What my experience has done is move me towards understanding, something I am forever seeking.

When I was a young man, I believed there must be something about the world, I, and other blacks didn't understand. The questions I was asking were, "Why is it that whites hate blacks," and "why is it that blacks appear to be in a perpetual state of oppression?"

I wanted to know why it seemed as if our condition never really improved from generation to generation. I concluded that there must be something that other people knew or understood that we Blacks, must not know or understand about the world. I grew up in a Christian home and attended a Baptist church, where I can recall riding the Sunday school bus as a child. But by the time I would begin my journey to try to understand the world, I had put the Bible down as irrelevant, though it is anything but.

I've always had a passion for learning and began by studying history. I would actually study many subjects, including science, and the more I understood about the world the more it brought me back to the Bible. Only now, I was looking at the Bible with new eyes and a different understanding. I now believe I couldn't get the right answers because I wasn't asking the right questions. The questions I had about the world, the Bible, and our condition were a result of the lies I'd been taught about the world and the people around me. I saw the world the way I had been taught to see the world.

The TRUTH that I'm going to share will, for many, be abrasive. That's because many of us have made decisions unknowingly to contribute to the current condition of the world. All races—Blacks, Whites, and Asians have participated in the destruction of the Black nation, Black family, and Black condition. The problem however is not exclusive to the Black Family. The destruction of the Black community is just a smaller part of a bigger problem that requires the attention of the entire world.

We as Blacks differ in our experiences and what we believe we need to do to move forward because we have a different understanding and vastly different life experiences. Although we have differences, there is but one truth. I have intentionally set out to make this as short as possible by not trying to answer all your questions but attempting to have you reread the Bible with new eyes and a more accurate worldview.

It's About Blood, Not Race

It's not about race, but the demonic bloodline. As I already stated, I grew up a poor kid in Cincinnati, Ohio. I eventually asked the question: why do white people hate black people? But I was asking the questions the way the world was taught to me. I don't see it that way anymore. Instead, I see the conflict as between the godly and godless, demonic people. One example is the BLM movement. It is a demonic communist organization, and it is using people to keep blacks and whites divided.

Homosexuality is a tool of the godless. I do not advocate for persecuting a person because of so-called sexual orientation, but I do see the rise of the gay pride movement and the politically correct efforts to "normalize" what God has not made normal as a way to weaken our moral and spiritual integrity as a society.

Interracial relationships between black people and white are not supposed to happen according to God's plan. Harmony between races, especially among the children of God of each race is a beautiful thing, but that does not require integration.

Integration is an idea of communism, and this supposed "unity" flies in the face of God's call for separateness. Integration forces different groups of people together so that it can tear them apart. Integration is infiltration and allows the enemy of God's people to sow tares among the wheat. Forcing people together who have different views, beliefs, and cultures creates more hostility than harmony. Left alone these groups would find their natural balance and learn to live among one another. The true goal of integration is infiltration. Integration, as it pertains to whites and blacks in America, was sold as an attempt to create equality for blacks. The truth of integration was that it did not allow blacks to live and move freely among whites, but was a tool to allow the Satanic to move among God's children. It was never about white and black.

Integration has not improved the relationships between our communities in America. What was integration for the black community is what we call globalization today for America. If you want to see America's future you need to only look at America's black community. After integration, the black economy began to crash. The money that once circulated in the black community left and the businesses it supported left with it. This is what has happened and is currently happening in America. American businesses followed American dollars right out of the country and those entrusted with protecting Americans from enemies foreign and domestic allowed it to happen, enriching themselves and their families. All races have within them those who are willing to deal with the devil.

> **[5] Only if thou carefully hearken unto the voice of the LORD thy God, to observe to do all these commandments which I command thee this day. [6] For the LORD thy God blesseth thee, as he promised thee: and thou shalt lend unto many nations, but thou shalt not borrow; and thou shalt reign over many nations, but they shall not reign over thee. (Deut 15:5-6, KJV)**

Only God knows all the reasons he has called for separateness in the design, but one obvious reason is that it is the best way to avoid the beasts among us. Whites are supposed to stay within their group and effectively deal with any disobedience to God among them. Traditions and customs of arranged marriages kept God's people's blood from mixing with the godless people for centuries.

Knowing your tribe is to know not only those who look like you, but believe like you, and worship the same God as you. Your tribe should be full of other people who believe like you.

Currently, Blacks and Whites exist in an environment where the Satanic control local government, courts, news, and media, and agitate both to keep us divided. The Satanic have used loyal Blacks to expand government and promote violent and Godless ideas, and they have used loyal Whites to perpetuate racism and division. These Godless people do not represent those who may look like them. Black Lives Matter does not represent God-fearing Blacks and Klansmen don't represent God-fearing Whites. Each race must effectively deal with those who would interfere with our ability to become allies of one another for God and freedom. If Blacks oppose the Klan or Whites oppose BLM, it is those conflicts that the Satanists use to manipulate our division. The enemy of God's people has learned from history what God's people are capable of if they ever become united. The tactic of divide and conquer has divided America by race, age, religion, and political affiliation. The rights of the Godly have been diminished, while the behavior and promotion of disobedience to God have grown. This is the eve of the fall. This is how all great civilizations end. We are in a cultural war—a war by deception.

Good vs. Evil

Consistent with the Creator's design of the world are the issues that all Americans face, Black and White, and they are the same issues that exist around the world.

We cannot deal effectively with these problems, because we deal with them using the false narrative we were given, which existed before many of us were born. White supremacy and institutionalized, or systemic racism are ideas given to us and perpetuated by the news and entertainment industry, controlled by a handful of corporations, and an education system controlled by the state.

> *The press must grow day in and day out. It is our Party's sharpest and most powerful weapon.*
>
> — **Joseph Stalin**

If we continue to address the problems in America and abroad using this narrative, we'll never move forward in dealing effectively with what's wrong with America.

Blacks in America aren't dealing with racism. We're dealing with Satanism, which is evil. We're dealing with evil supremacy and institutionalized evil. The evil that exists in America affects everyone. Financially, whites have been the beneficiary of these ideas because they divide, which is what was intended. It is wealth that can and will be taken under socialism/communism. This wealth is already being taken. Now that Satanists have effectively destroyed the black community and family, they have turned their attention toward white America.

Blacks and Whites in America have failed to deal with the weeds among them. The blood that flowed through the veins of those Africans who sold Africans, and the blood of Europeans who bought enslaved people are still among us. Slavery and oppression are still being practiced by those who are not God's people.

Bolshevism is an idea our ancestors understood, which is why men like John Brown and other Northerners fought against slavery and the south. Northern Whites in America didn't fight for the freedom of Blacks, contrary to the current narrative. They fought for their freedom. Liberty has always unified God's people regardless of nationality. Our ancestors understood what slavery represented and what it meant for the future of America.

Today, Americans have forgotten. We point at each other while allowing those who wish to destroy god-fearing Blacks and god-fearing Whites to flourish. It's not white privilege. It's an evil privilege. It's the Satanic/Godless who hold seats of power in America's political system, both White and Black. Satanic men and women control the images on our television and promote Satanic education.

Satanist kill Blacks in the inner-city and say it's Black on Black when most of it isn't. These are the same people who are making it harder to feed and house America's families.

We can't effectively deal with the problem if we don't change the narrative.

It was not racists who distributed crack cocaine drugs in the inner-cities of America. These were evil people. These same Satanic people are now spreading dope in white middle-class communities, devastating their communities and destroying the population of rural America.

All Americans receive the same Satanic television programming and socialist/ pro-choice education. Leaded water flows through the pipes of American homes throughout the country, and all Americans pay high prices for food, gas, and housing.

Blacks wrongly labeled their problems as racist, incorrectly communicating to other Americans that the issues we're dealing with require a big government solution. This is precisely what the enemy of God's people wanted us to do. Misguided by miseducated leaders, Blacks were led to the tree for answers. That tree represents big government/communism, and each time we went there, we were given an apple, and we did eat it. We ate off the integration apple, feminism apple, equality apple, civil rights apple, homosexuality apple, and the voting rights apple.

Blacks and Whites in America, both men, and women have been used to move forward ideas of integration, homosexuality, and feminism. The children today have to deal with their parents' choices in the same way Abel had to deal with the decisions of Adam and Eve.

The leaders of BLM are no different than the Africans who sold enslaved people. They represent their financial interest. The Black church has not moved our community towards independence. They also represent their financial interests. The same holds for the so-called religious leaders of Black Americans, past and present. None of their solutions to America's problems were Biblical solutions. Marching, protesting, voting, and boycotting aren't Biblical solutions. The Black church pushed for integration and equality. These are socialist ideas.

The truth of this is evident in the history of Black communities. Before Blacks in America went to the tree. They had strong families and growing communities. Blacks were creating their wealth. The violence and the absence of black men in large numbers of homes didn't exist. Communities like that in Tulsa, OK existed before integration, before women's lib, and before civil rights. The barriers to voting for Blacks weren't removed until 1965.

So how is it that Blacks post-slavery were able to do more, with less education and supposedly fewer freedoms?

The reason is that they were living the way God intended, and Blacks were beginning to reap the benefits of obedience. Our grandparents were being fruitful and multiplying and dealt with the weeds among them. It wasn't until Blacks went to the tree that we began to fall away from God.

Voting isn't in the Bible, because that's not what God told you to do. The Creator didn't tell Moses to integrate, and the Creator has not instructed us to liberate our women and feminize our men. I have not found in history that people have delivered themselves by voting. However, history has shown that if people vote long enough, they will eventually vote themselves into communism or fascism, which is a condition they will have to shoot themselves out of. The examples here are Hitler and Lenin.

The leaders of Black Americans past and present have been educated socialists, and like the leaders of BLM today, they have sworn allegiance to communism.

The best way to control the opposition is to lead it ourselves.

— **Vladimir Lenin**

Whites are responsible for dealing with the weeds in their garden because these men and women we have called racists will also do these things to whites. Satanist do not value life here in America or anywhere else in the world. This helps understand the current war between Ukraine and Russia, two countries that were one nation. Who are now shooting at each other. It's always Good vs. Evil.

Once we correctly identify the problem, we can begin to deal with what's wrong with America and what's wrong with the world.

The solution to the problems facing God's people is in the Bible. This means no matter how great the struggle Blacks believe they have, once God's people decide that they want the world to change, they only need to decide to change it.

Lions of God do not have to convince the Hyenas of Satan to be anything other than what they are. God's people only have to decide to be the Lions he created. You can not legislate a snake to be something other than a snake.

God's people have to do what Moses did: walk away from evil and live the way the Creator commanded. Even then, God made them wait for forty years so that there remained none among them who weren't worthy to enter the Promised Land.

The truth the Bible is trying to convey is that to subdue the world, you must first conquer yourself. Conquering yourself is having self-restraint and refraining from doing the deeds of those around you. To be special, the Creator's children require standards. Those standards are the laws of the OT.

Once God's people decide they are ready, "He's" ready. The Creator doesn't do it for you, "He" does it with you.

The Creator is waiting on us.

Deuteronomy 30:2-3,5,7-9 KJV

> **[2] And shalt return unto the LORD thy God, and shalt obey his voice according to all that I command thee this day, thou and thy children, with all thine heart, and with all thy soul; [3] That then the LORD thy God will turn thy captivity, and have compassion upon thee, and will return and gather thee from all the nations, whither the LORD thy God hath scattered thee.**
>
> **[5] And the LORD thy God will bring thee into the land which thy fathers possessed, and thou shalt possess it; and he will do thee good, and multiply thee above thy fathers.**
>
> **[7] And the LORD thy God will put all these curses upon thine enemies, and on them that hate thee, which persecuted thee. [8] And thou shalt return and obey the voice of the LORD, and do all his commandments which I command thee this day. [9] And the LORD thy God will make thee plenteous in every work of thine hand, in the fruit of thy body, and in the fruit of thy cattle, and in the fruit of thy land, for good: for the LORD will again rejoice over thee for good, as he rejoiced over thy fathers**

Brother Against Brother

Genesis 4:8 says, "And Cain talked with Abel his brother: and it came to pass, when they were in the field, that Cain rose up against Abel his brother, and slew him" (KJV).

America's deadliest war was its Civil War, which pitted brother vs. brother. It is estimated that 650,000 men may have died in this war. Nearly as many men died in the American Civil War more than all of the other U.S. wars combined. Each race has the responsibility to deal effectively with the godless among them. America failed to rid itself of the ungodly and instead decided to negotiate with the devil.

13th Amendment

Amendment XIII Section 1 states,

> Neither slavery nor involuntary servitude, except as a punishment for a crime whereof the party shall have been duly convicted, shall exist within the United States, or any place subject to their jurisdiction.

The key word in this deal is "except", and what would follow is currently the world's largest prison population. Death and slavery are the markers of communism. In America, what we call White privilege is actually an ungodly privilege. Those who are white and black benefit from aligning themselves with communist ideology and satanic values.

The only successful slave rebellion to result in the forming of a nation happened in Haiti when black and brown slaves rebelled against their French oppressors and won their independence (although at a great spiritual and financial cost). Napoleon Bonaparte said this at the time:

> My decision to destroy the authority of the blacks in Saint Domingue (Haiti) is not so much based on considerations of commerce and money, as on the need to block the march of the blacks in the world forever.

Napoleon was unsuccessful, except that, while the slaves won Haiti, they ultimately were crushed into their current state of poverty and depravity by crippling reparations to the French government. Haitian leadership after fighting for their freedom made the mistake of thinking they could negotiate and normalize relationships with those who represent the beast.

Segregation Now, Segregation Forever

Every year during black history month, someone quotes George Wallace's 1963 speech blasting integration. They hold him up as an example of racism and oppression. I have printed the speech here. Read it, and I will have some comments at the end. Also, keep in mind that this speech was written for Wallace by Ku Klux Klansman, Asa Carter.

(1963) GEORGE WALLACE, "SEGREGATION NOW, SEGREGATION FOREVER"

POSTED ON JANUARY 22, 2013, AND CONTRIBUTED BY: BLACKPAST

George C Wallace, Alabama, February 8, 1968

Courtesy U.S. Library of Congress

By 1963 Alabama Governor George Corley Wallace had emerged as the leading opponent to the growing civil rights movement. Six months later he gained international notoriety for his stand in the door of the University of Alabama to block the entrance of two black students, Vivian Malone and James Hood, who had been ordered to be admitted by a federal judge. Between 1964 and 1976 Wallace ran for President four times (three as a Democrat and once as an Independent) exploiting what he believed was a deep-seated aversion to racial integration among Northerners as well as Southerners. Long before these events, he would at his inauguration as Governor on January 14, 1963, lay out his opposition to integration and the civil rights movement. His excerpted speech appears below.

> Today I have stood, where once Jefferson Davis stood and took an oath to my people. It is very appropriate than that from this Cradle of the Confederacy, this very Heart of the Great Anglo-Saxon Southland, that today we sound the drum for freedom as have our generations of forebears before us done, time and time again through history. Let us rise to the call of freedom-loving blood that is in us and send our answer to the tyranny that clanks its chains upon the South. In the name of the greatest people that have

ever trod this earth, I draw the line in the dust and toss the gauntlet before the feet of tyranny . . . and I say . . . segregation today . . . segregation tomorrow . . . segregation forever.

The Washington, D.C. school riot report is disgusting and revealing. We will not sacrifice our children to any such type of school system–and you can write that down. The federal troops in Mississippi could be better used guarding the safety of the citizens of Washington, D.C., where it is even unsafe to walk or go to a ballgame–and that is the nation's capital. I was safer in a B-29 bomber over Japan during the war in an air raid than the people of Washington are walking to the White House neighborhood. A closer example is Atlanta. The city officials fawn for political reasons over school integration and THEN build barricades to stop residential integration–what hypocrisy!

Let us send this message back to Washington by our representatives who are with us today– that from this day we are standing up, and the heel of tyranny does not fit the neck of an upright man . . . that we intend to take the offensive and carry our fight for freedom across the nation, wielding the balance of power we know we possess in the Southland . . . . that WE, not the insipid bloc of voters of some sections . . will determine in the next election who shall sit in the White House of these United States . . . That from this day, from this hour . . . from this minute . . . we give the word of a race of honor that we will tolerate their boot in our face no longer . . . . and let those certain judges put that in their opium pipes of power and smoke it for what it is worth.

Hear me, Southerners! You sons and daughters who have moved north and west throughout this nation . . . . we call on you from your native soil to join with us in national support and vote . . and we know . . . wherever you are . . away from the hearths of the Southland . . . that you will respond, for though you may live in the farthest reaches of this vast country . . . . your heart has never left Dixieland.

And you native sons and daughters of old New England's rock-ribbed patriotism . . . and you sturdy natives of the great Mid-West . . and you descendants of the far West flaming spirit of pioneer freedom . . we invite you to come and be with us . . for you are of the Southern spirit . . and the Southern philosophy . . . you are Southerners too and brothers with us in our fight.

What I have said about segregation goes double this day . . . and what I have said to or about some federal judges goes TRIPLE this day…

And while the manufacturing industries of free enterprise have been coming to our state in increasing numbers, attracted by our bountiful natural resources, our growing numbers of skilled workers, and our favorable conditions, their present rate of settlement here can be increased from the trickle they now represent to a stream of enterprise and endeavor, capital and expansion that can join us in our work of development and enrichment of the educational futures of our children, the opportunities of our citizens and the fulfillment of our talents as God has given them to us. To realize our ambitions and to bring to fruition our dreams, we as Alabamians must take cognizance of the world about us. We must re-define our heritage, and re-school our thoughts in the lessons our forefathers knew so well, firsthand, in order to function, grow and prosper. We can no longer hide our head in the sand and tell ourselves that the ideology of our free fathers is not being attacked and is not being threatened by another idea . . . for it is. We are faced with an idea that if a centralized government assumes enough authority, enough power over its people, that it can provide a utopian life . . that if given the power to dictate, to forbid, to require, to demand, to distribute, to edict and to judge what is best and enforce that will produce only "good" . . and it shall be our father . . . . and our God. . . .

We find we have replaced faith with fear . . . and though we may give lip service to the Almighty . . in reality, the government has become our god. It is, therefore, a basically ungodly government, and its appeal to the pseudo-intellectual and the politician is to change their status from servant of the people to master of the people . . . to play at being God . . . without faith in God . . . and without the wisdom of God. It is a system that is the very opposite of Christ for it feeds and encourages everything degenerate and based in our people as it assumes the responsibilities that we ourselves should assume. Its pseudo-liberal spokesmen and some Harvard advocates have never examined the logic of its substitution of what it calls "human rights" for individual rights, for its propaganda play on words, has to appeal for the unthinking. Its logic is totally material and irresponsible as it runs the full gamut of human desires . . . including the theory that everyone has voting rights without the spiritual responsibility of preserving freedom. Our founding fathers recognized those rights . . . but only within the framework of those spiritual responsibilities. But the strong, simple faith and sane reasoning of our founding fathers have long since been forgotten as the so-called "progressives" tell us that our Constitution was written for "horse and buggy" days . . . so were the Ten Commandments.

Not so long ago men stood in marvel and awe at the cities, the buildings, the schools, the autobahns that the government of Hitler's Germany had built . . . just as centuries before they stood in wonder of Rome's building . . . but it could not stand . . . for the system that built it had rotted the souls of the builders . . . and in turn . . . rotted the foundation of what God meant that men should be. Today that same system on an international scale is sweeping the world. It is the "changing world" of which we are told . . . it is called "new" and "liberal". It is as old as the oldest dictator. It is degenerate and decadent. As the national racism of Hitler's Germany persecuted a national minority to the whim of a national majority . . . so the international racism of the liberals seek to persecute the international white minority to the whim of the international colored majority . . . so that we are footballed about according to the favor of the Afro-Asian bloc. But the Belgian survivors of the Congo cannot present their case to a war crimes commission . . . nor the Portuguese of Angola . . . nor the survivors of Castro . . . nor the citizens of Oxford, Mississippi.

It is this theory of international power politic that led a group of men on the Supreme Court for the first time in American history to issue an edict, based not on legal precedent, but upon a volume, the editor of which said our Constitution is outdated and must be changed and the writers of which, some had admittedly belonged to as many as half a hundred communist-front organizations. It is this theory that led this same group of men to briefly bare the ungodly core of that philosophy in forbidding little school children to say a prayer. And we found evidence of that ungodliness even in the removal of the words "in God we trust" from some of our dollars, which was placed there as evidence by our founding fathers as the faith upon which this system of government was built. It is the spirit of power thirst that caused a President in Washington to take up Caesar's pen and with one stroke of it make a law. A Law which the law-making body of Congress refused to pass . . . a law that tells us that we can or cannot buy or sell our very homes, except by his conditions . . . and except at HIS discretion. It is the spirit of power thirst that led the same President to launch a full offensive of twenty-five thousand troops against a university . . . of all places . . . in his own country . . . and against his own people, when this nation maintains only six thousand troops in the beleaguered city of Berlin. We have witnessed such acts of "might makes right" over the world as men yielded to the temptation to play God . . . but we have never before witnessed it in America. We reject such acts as free men. We do not defy, for there is nothing to defy . . . since as free men we do not recognize any government right to give freedom . . . or deny freedom. No government erected by man has that right. As Thomas Jefferson said, "The God who gave us life, gave us liberty at the same time; no King holds the right of liberty in his hands." Nor does any ruler in the American government....

We intend, quite simply, to practice the free heritage as bequeathed to us as sons of free fathers. We intend to re-vitalize the truly new and progressive form of government that is less than two hundred years old . . . a government first founded in this nation simply and purely on faith . . . that there is a personal God who rewards good and punishes evil . . . that hard work will receive its just deserts . . . that ambition and ingenuity and inventiveness . . . and profit of such . . .are admirable traits and goals . . . that the individual is encouraged in his spiritual growth and from that growth arrives at a character that enhances his charity toward others and from that character and that charity so is influenced business, and labor and farmer and government. We intend to renew our faith as God-fearing men . . . not government-fearing men nor any other kind of fearing-men. We intend to roll up our sleeves and pitch in to develop this full bounty God has given us . . . to live full and useful lives and in absolute freedom from all fear. Then can we enjoy the full richness of the Great American Dream. . . .

This nation was never meant to be a unit of one . . . but a united of the many . . . . that is the exact reason our freedom-loving forefathers established the states, so as to divide the rights and powers among the states, ensuring that no central power could gain master government control.

In united effort we were meant to live under this government . . . whether Baptist, Methodist, Presbyterian, Church of Christ, or whatever one's denomination or religious belief . . . each respecting the other's right to a separate denomination . . . each, by working to develop his own, enriching the total of all our lives through a united effort. And so it was meant in our political lives . . . whether Republican, Democrat, Prohibition or whatever political party . . . each striving from his separate political station . . . respecting the rights of others to be separate and work from within their political framework . . . and each separate political station making its contribution to our lives . . . .

And so it was meant in our racial lives . . . each race, within its own framework has the freedom to teach . . to instruct . . to develop . . to ask for and receive deserved help from others of separate racial stations. This is the great freedom of our American founding fathers . . . but if we amalgamate into the one unit as advocated by the communist philosophers . . . then the enrichment of our lives . . . the freedom for our development . . . is gone forever. We become, therefore, a mongrel unit of one under a single all-powerful government . . . and we stand for everything . . . and for nothing.

The true brotherhood of America, of respecting the separateness of others . . . and uniting in the effort . . . have been so twisted and distorted from its original concept that there is a small wonder that communism is winning the world.

We invite the negro citizens of Alabama to work with us from his separate racial station . . . as we will work with him . . . to develop, to grow in individual freedom and enrichment. We want jobs and a good future for BOTH races . . . the tubercular and the infirm. This is the basic heritage of my religion, of which I make full practice . . . . for we are all the handiwork of God.

But we warn those, of any group, who would follow the false doctrine of communistic amalgamation that we will not surrender our system of government . . . our freedom of race and religion . . . that freedom was won at a hard price and if it requires a hard price to retain it . . . we are able . . . and quite willing to pay it.

The liberals' theory that poverty, discrimination, and lack of opportunity is the cause of communism is a false theory . . . if it were true the South would have been the biggest single communist bloc in the western hemisphere long ago . . . for after the great War Between the States, our people faced a desolate land of burned universities, destroyed crops and homes, with manpower depleted and crippled, and even the mule, which was required to work the land, was so scarce that whole communities shared one animal to make the spring plowing. There were no government handouts, no Marshall Plan aid, and no coddling to make sure that our people would not suffer; instead, the South was set upon by the vulturous carpetbagger and federal troops, and all loyal Southerners were denied the vote at the point of the bayonet so that the infamous, illegal 14th Amendment might be passed. There was no money, no food, and no hope of either. But our grandfathers bent their knee only in church and bowed their head only to God. . . .

We remind all within hearing of this Southland that a Southerner, Peyton Randolph, presided over the Continental Congress in our nation's beginning . . . that a Southerner, Thomas Jefferson, wrote the Declaration of Independence, that a Southerner, George Washington, is the Father of our country . . . that a Southerner, James Madison, authored our Constitution, that a Southerner, George Mason, authored the Bill of Rights and it was a Southerner who said, "Give me liberty . . . . . . or give me death," Patrick Henry.

Southerners played a most magnificent part in erecting this great divinely inspired system of freedom . . . and as God is our witness, Southerners will save it.

Let us, as Alabamians, grasp the hand of destiny and walk out of the shadow of fear . . . and fill our divine destination. Let us not simply defend . . . but let us assume the leadership of the fight and carry our leadership across this

> nation. God has placed us here in this crisis . . . let us not fail in this . . . our most historical moment.

In an attempt to follow the truth wherever it leads. I thought it necessary to understand why men like Marcus Garvey and Fred Hampton would have set down with the KKK an organization with a history of violence towards Blacks. What becomes clear is that both Blacks and Whites are in a condition where we have both forgotten our history.

We've done something in America that people in many parts of the world don't do. We consider everyone in America either White, Black, Hispanic or Asian. We don't distinguish each group as German, Italian, Turkish, Japanese, or Chinese we tend to group everyone in one large group. The problem is that the enemy doesn't see us that way. Romans understand that not all whites are the same and they are interested in destroying Africans as well as Barbarians. Barbarians are any Whites who are not Roman. Barbarians would have been the term they were referred to preceding and during the time of Jesus. It is a term that was meant by the Romans to be derogatory.

What does this have to do with George Wallace?

The truth which becomes uncomfortable is that he was correct. One doesn't have to agree with every single one of Wallace's sentiments to see that on some points, he makes logical sense. He said that integration was a tool of communism. This is absolutely true. Why? Because communism is collectivism. Collectivism has no regard for the individual, but only for whatever the group is trying to control. When we value the individual as the smallest sacred minority, then we value his right to partner with whomever he wishes, *and to refuse to partner with whomever he wishes.*

The problem is whom Wallace associated himself with. There may have very well been Klansmen who shared Wallace's beliefs, but having Romans among them, they would use a sound byte from George Wallace's speech, "segregation today . . . segregation tomorrow . . . segregation forever", along with violence to undermine any attempts of success.

The mistake Wallace made is the same mistake Whites and Blacks are making today. We assume because they look like us, they're not against us. President Obama went to African countries pushing for homosexuality. Also, under President Obama, Muammar Gaddafi was killed, a man who wanted a United Africa. Gaddafi also wanted an African currency that was backed by African resources. Yet, still today many Blacks still support him.

Wallace made the mistake of not following his own beliefs of segregation by separating himself again from those who do not believe what he believes.

What today's Romans couldn't allow, is Africans and Barbarians to unite again on American soil. History reminds them of what happens when God's people unite. Hannibal Barca from Carthage, Northern Africa united Barbarians and marched towards Rome, at the time the Roman army was the world's mightiest.

Hannibal Barca would lead a united army through the Alps at a time when many believed it was impassable and defeat the Roman army in battle. What we have is a war that has continued and has always existed. A battle between good and evil. The deception has become more sophisticated with advances in technology but the parties remain the same.

So when men like Fred Hampton and Marcus Garvey sat with the KKK, they understood what great leaders understood and that is understanding what commonality we have that can unite and make allies of us. That uniting force is liberty. God's children have to deal with the same devil.

The devil's response to Wallace's words, he was shot and paralyzed in 1972. Marcus Garvey was exiled in 1927, Malcolm X whose parents were Garveyites was killed in 1965, Fred Hampton was killed in 1969 and once Malcolm X convinced Martin Luther King that he was wrong about integration, he was killed in 1968.

In the 1960's we also saw the murder of JFK, and interstates and highways ripped through and destroyed Black communities and businesses throughout the country. An expansion of welfare required the removal of men and the feminist movement. Since then we have seen the degradation of America, American families, values, and communities.

Many years after Wallace made his infamous speech, The NY Times featured an article about him. Here are some quotes from a <u>NY</u>

<u>Times article:</u>

> Starting in 1979, he also undertook a campaign of apology and revisionist explanation intended to erase the word "racist" from his epitaph.
>
> He argued that his early devotion to segregation was based on his reading of the Constitution and the Bible and was misinterpreted as a racist hatred of black people.
>
> "I made a mistake in the sense that I should have clarified my position more," he said in his last term as a Governor. "I was never saying anything that reflected upon black people, and I'm very sorry it was taken that way."

Wallace shows that he held no animosity towards black people. He seemed to want them to prosper as much as whites. What he tried to convey was the very idea that I am proposing, God, who called his people to shun the mixing of fabrics, loves separation. It is a principle that runs through the entire OT.

This shows that Wallace was certainly not perfect in his understanding, but I am not saying that he was. I am not saying that he completely understood black people. I am only saying that he understood the relationship between integration and communism. The problem is that the nuances of this are difficult to grasp because people viewed him as racist—and racism is ugly and wrong—his ideas on segregation were dismissed.

I mention this because today there is a nearly impossible challenge ahead. I must make the case for separation based on the ideal of individualism. All men are created equally. That is, all the children of God are created equally, but God has separated them into ethnicities and cultures.

No group should oppress another. The abomination that was slavery was not the separateness, but the oppression, the use of force to curtail the rights of a race. That was wrong, evil, and rightly done away with. The same goes for Jim Crow laws of segregation. But if we could have been allowed to be separate but truly equal, we would have thrived, without a doubt.

But the communist principles of integration and welfare have done tremendous harm to blacks in America. Why are these communist principles? Because when you integrate, you are trying to take away all differences in order to make one man. That one man is a follower and worshiper of the state, the collective. This is not a biblical ideal. It is satanic. The welfare state promises to bring "equality." What it brings instead is weakness, dependence, fatherlessness, and government control.

> *It's not an endlessly expanding list of rights — the "right" to education, the "right" to health care, the "right" to food and housing. That's not freedom, that's dependency. Those aren't rights, those are the rations of slavery — hay and a barn for human cattle.*
>
> -**P.J. O'Rourke**

As of this writing (2022), the Supreme Court just struck down Roe v. Wade. Aside from the illogical and satanic cries of oppression towards women, millions are clamoring now for an expansion of welfare. Even conservatives in virtue signaling are calling for "taking care of the babies that will be born and their mothers." This sounds so loving. It sounds so Christlike. But it is satanic and will lead us further down the road toward communism. Even Wallace, a democrat, missed the connection between welfare and communism.

Integration isn't about Blacks being able to live among Whites, that's the deception. Integration is allowing the godless to live among the godly. Let me state it again. There is not anything wrong with segregation, but it is actually a biblical concept. This is not white supremacy or even black supremacy. I prefer my tribe, Because I am black, I prefer blacks to whites. This is because I prefer myself to others. I don't mean that we should not be humble, I simply mean that there is no one else on earth who is supposed to prioritize my life, except for me. We are all given our lives to steward. I prefer myself because it is logical to do so. I am the first person I must feed. If the plane loses altitude, I am supposed to put my own mask on first, because how can I help the child in the seat next to me if I'm dead?

Beyond that, I must prioritize my family, then my extended family, my community, and then my tribe. God had grouped us as communities of individuals in part for the sake of thriving, and in part for the sake of maintaining purity, and preventing the evil, the satanic from living among us.

I believe what the enemy has done is to make it uncomfortable for either race to feel proud of their community without associating it with racism. What I'm trying to communicate is that there is a third party at play and Blacks and Whites have the same enemy. It is not racist for Whites to love Whites. It's not racist for either group to do what they believe is best for their community. What we both must recognize is that neither can defend America alone. Anything that divides us is a threat to both. We cannot be allies of one another if we don't learn how to live alongside one another and that requires us to simply respect one another's differences.

The programming for Blacks is so bad that there are many Blacks who feel if they do anything independent of Whites they are being racist. The problem with this ideology is that it promotes and seeks big government to solve our problems instead of solving them ourselves. Which in turn creates friction between Whites and Blacks. Whites having, I believe, an estimated 40x more wealth than Blacks, typically do not want big government. Actually, anyone who is financially stable doesn't want a big government.

Everything has been weaponized to divide. Caring about your race, community, and family should never be looked upon as racist or bad. The only thing that is evil is when *either interferes with another person's ability to do the same.*

Globalism

Today, there is a new iteration of this same demonic problem. What integration was for Blacks, globalization is for Americans. If you take a step back and look at America, you'll be able to see it. Integration is really disintegration. What America did to the black community is what Communists are doing to America. The Black community lost control of its own schools, communities, businesses, entertainment, and its whole economy.

Both Whites and Blacks contributed to the destruction of the Black community and America. This destruction is biblical because the Bible warns that these things will happen in diverse places.

Matthew 24:7-12

> **For nation shall rise against nation, and kingdom against kingdom: and there shall be famines, and pestilences, and earthquakes, in divers places. [8] All these are the beginning of sorrows. [9] Then shall they deliver you up to be afflicted, and shall kill you: and ye shall be hated of all nations for my name's sake. [10] And then shall many be offended, and shall betray one another, and shall hate one another. [11] And many false prophets shall rise, and shall deceive many. [12] And because iniquity shall abound, the love of many shall wax cold.**

So what is globalism? Globalism has many nuances to its meaning, but at heart, it is the idea that what we should be working toward is a one-world government. For centuries, what hindered globalization was distance and cultural distinctions. But distance is no longer a factor, not just because of supersonic air travel, but because of the even faster speed of the internet and the entertainment industry. Lines are becoming blurrier and blurrier between people groups and cultures. Consider right now the meteoric rise of K-Pop, the Korean music groups, usually "boy bands" that are a sensation all over the world, including in America. The phenomenon of the "boy band" started in America, made its way to Asia, and then came back to America, but with the Asians. The only next step is a more multicultural boy band, with red and yellow, black and white, and don't forget a trans person or two in the next version!

To be sure, not everyone who advocates for some measure of globalism is vying for a one-world government. Some simply want open borders and free trade between countries. Some of this would be good for everyone, but just as the erasure of the individual would have catastrophic consequences, so would the erasure of that individual's culture and home.

What would happen if there was only one government? What would it be like to live in a world where there was no escape from a corrupt state? Not only is this unbiblical, but it is unlivable. A group of individuals needs a country with a government and an army to stand up for the individuals in that state against other countries who would not respect their freedoms but will respect their strength together.

It's About the Beasts

But the most important issue in all of this is that in order to effectively monitor ourselves and our societies to identify the Beast among us, we must stay primarily within our tribe. Just as Black (and White) Americans lost the ability to police their own by integrating, we all will lose our ability to monitor ourselves with the onslaught of globalism. God did not call us to globalism. That was tried in Bible times, and the results were catastrophic. In Genesis 11 it says:

> **11 And the whole earth was of one language, and of one speech.**
>
> **2 And it came to pass, as they journeyed from the east, that they found a plain in the land of Shinar; and they dwelt there.**
>
> **3 And they said one to another, Go to, let us make brick, and burn them thoroughly. And they had brick for stone, and slime had them for mortar.**

4 And they said, Go to, let us build us a city and a tower, whose top may reach unto heaven; and let us make us a name, lest we be scattered abroad upon the face of the whole earth.

5 And the Lord came down to see the city and the tower, which the children of men builded.

6 And the Lord said, Behold, the people is one, and they have all one language; and this they begin to do: and now nothing will be restrained from them, which they have imagined to do.

7 Go to, let us go down, and there confound their language, that they may not understand one another's speech.

8 So the Lord scattered them abroad from thence upon the face of all the earth: and they left off to build the city.

9 Therefore is the name of it called Babel; because the Lord did there confound the language of all the earth: and from thence did the Lord scatter them abroad upon the face of all the earth.

What was it that God told Adam? Did he tell him to populate the earth? What did he tell Noah? Genesis 9:1 says, "And God blessed Noah and his sons, and said unto them, Be fruitful, and multiply, **and replenish the earth**" (KJV emphasis added). But instead, they wanted to stay all together as one mighty nation, to make themselves "a name." The Lord scattered them because he would have his way.

The created world belongs to God, and He gave it to his children to maintain. In order for Satan and his followers to steal what belongs to God and His children, he needs the authority of a big government, which is communism. Again, the purpose of the Bible is that God's children will know how to live freely.

This is what the story of the Tower of Babel represents. This story is read as literal, in that man sought to build a physical tower to heaven. But it is not meant to be taken literally. It is suggesting what's currently in conversation and that's a one-world order. The biblical meaning of the tower that we're looking for is to surpass God.

Satan and his followers seek to surpass God and tower over His authority here on earth. Isaiah tells us what Satan says, "I will ascend above the heights of the clouds; I will be like the most High" (Isa 14:14 KJV).

This is just one of many dualities that exist in the world: big family vs big government. There's another more fundamental duality that's connected to this. There exist two world orders. One order represents Life and freedom and the other represents Death and slavery.

In 1991 George H.W. Bush, on the first 9/11 in his State of the Union speech before the joint sessions of Congress, announced that we were moving towards a one world order. I waited for someone to ask, "Is this one world order under democracy, which is Life and freedom, or communism, which is death and slavery." No one asked. No one ever asked what comes next, children never do.

> **[28] For they are a nation void of counsel, neither is there any understanding in them. [29] O that they were wise, that they understood this, that they would consider their latter end! (Deut 32:28-29 KJV)**

What came 10 years later is the second 9/11 and now George W. Bush, Jr is in office. We all watched the ceremony of death, which was the fall of the Twin Towers. The fall of a two-world order system and the rise of a one-world order system represent the rise of communism. The ceremony was the fall of the twin towers that represent the two peoples of the earth and a celebration of what grew from the ashes, that those two towers represented, the One World Trade Center. America's very own tower of Babel.

So what can be done about globalism? Do we need God to send persecution? Do we need him to confuse our language and scatter us? Do we need him to divide us in every way except one? I am not advocating that any nation should oppress another nation. Nations, that is, individuals who have banded together in a region with a government, should treat each other the way individuals should treat each other—honestly, mutually respectful, but understanding themselves as separate entities. And then, within those nations of individuals, the children of God should worship together and be equipped to fight satanic evil in their midst. The serpent will come into any nation with his lies and temptations to follow the ways of death and darkness, offering the "knowledge" of good and evil. Can the children of God source out who has partaken of that fruit? Can they recognize the serpent when he is crawling on his belly in their midst? That's what we aim to find out, and that's what God calls his children to do—-before it is too late.

Shun Distractions

On a side note, I think that's why we have social media platforms like Tik Tok. They are making us waste time while we're losing our freedoms and our country. Scrolling mindlessly through Facebook, Instagram, and Twitter, is zapping productive energy, and when they are not destroying our brain cells and capacity to concentrate, they are outraging us with the algorithms and well-placed information bombs, sure to get us to click, respond, like, or dislike, keeping their machine running and our minds incapacitated.

The main distraction for the last hundred years has been the race war. This is what the enemy would have us focus on. The problem for blacks is whites. The problem for whites is blacks, and the problem for both is Asians, or browns, or the Taliban! But this is a ruse to get us to hate and kill each other, rather than focus on the true source of our destruction: Evil. The Beasts are among us. When we can stop believing the lie that we are victims of some race because of our race, and realize that satan is our true enemy, then we can work together with other separate nations to create the world God called us to create.

How do we defeat him? First, we must look at his works and destroy his works. Race wars are his work. Race riots are his work. Communism is his work, and the sort of integration that is an erasing of cultures is his work. Anything satan can do to undermine God's ways, especially when it comes to the way God has designed governments to flourish, he will do. Eroding the sovereignty and free will, first of individuals, then of states, is Satan's work.

Do not be distracted. Step one is to love freedom and love your own people. Step two is to look within your group for those who live and lead others to live according to the ways of the "tree of knowledge." Make no place for them in your societies. Turn to God and his Word and seek his kingdom, his righteousness, and the ways he promised would lead to life and not death. Let the beast pursue death, but don't let us go along with him.

Chapter 5

Education and Miseducation

Once you lose your God, you lose your mind. Once you've lost your mind, you lose your freedom.

Today, man has done what most civilizations before him have done, and we've eaten of the Tree of the Knowledge of Good and Evil. It appears that Man is able to unravel the mysteries of the world and bring forth technologies and sciences, which allow him to do all things. The problem is, once introduced, you won't know the difference between what is good and what is evil. You begin to move further away from God. This is where man currently is today. **The knowledge he has gained has done what it was intended to do. It has brought forth confusion and chaos in a world that is supposed to maintain order and structure.** We currently debate gender neutrality and argue for and against non-binary gender. **Today, education is not about learning it's about indoctrination. Its intention is to mold God's children into someone who is disobedient to God.**

Education is a weapon the effect of which is determined by the hands which wield it, by who is to be struck down.

-Joseph Stalin

Give me your four year olds, and in a generation I will build a socialist state.

-Vladimir Lenin

Give me just one generation of youth, and I'll transform the whole world.

-Vladimir Lenin

Give me a child for the first 5 years of his life and he will be mine forever.

-Vladimir Lenin

Perfect Definition of Atheist Dogma. Your mind has been subjected to subtle mental conditioning year after year. Now the atheist lie has become the truth to you. A lie that can be blown away with the real truth. It just takes time to unwind the atheist mental conditioning. The truth is out there. Outside of atheist dogma lies the truth!

-Vladimir Lenin

Can a nation be free if it oppresses other nations? It cannot.

-Vladimir Lenin

Keep people from their history, and they are easily controlled.

-Karl Marx

My object in life is to dethrone God and destroy capitalism.

-Karl Marx

Take away a nation's heritage and they are more easily persuaded.

-Karl Marx

The education of all children, from the moment that they can get along without a mother's care, shall be in state institutions.

-Karl Marx

Communism begins where atheism begins.

-Karl Marx

If you can cut the people off from their history, then they can be easily persuaded.

-Karl Marx

We know that violent measures against religion are nonsense, but this is an opinion: as socialism grows, religion will disappear. Its disappearance must be done by social development, in which education must play a part.

-Karl Marx

Don't get me wrong. I believe that discovery is in the nature of man. What history reveals is that the greatest minds the world has produced were those of godly people. I'm not talking about those people who made small contributions to man. I'm talking about your Teslas and George Washington Carvers men who credited their discoveries, not to their own genius, but to God revealing to them these inventions.

The point of this is that Creation is Life, and Life is Creation. Free men and women that possess Life create. Communist countries, where people are not free, have contributed very little to the modern world. And if something doesn't change about our modern education system, we will see less and less of this God-given creative capacity as our children are inundated with the Knowledge of Good and Evil, rather than Truth.

So how does our current public education system undermine the people of God and create followers for Satan? What is so pernicious about knowledge is that it turns one from God? Is all knowledge evil? No, all knowledge is not the wretched, "Knowledge of Good and Evil." For instance, I have come to my conclusions by way of my study of the *knowledge* of history. In doing so, I have come to God and the Bible.

But consider our education system and its purposes. In America and other parts of the world, the public education system has been profoundly shaped by John Dewey (1859-1952), whose progressive idea (and I am somewhat overgeneralizing) was that the role of the school was not to educate children but to socialize them and teach them to be good citizens. Doesn't that sound grand? But Dewey was a socialist, if not a communist, and his system and philosophy were designed to create an egalitarian, socialist society, which is only the tiniest baby step away from a communist society.

Therefore, the so-called "knowledge" taught in his schools is not the facts or conceptual truth about how God made the world, but rather, it is about group projects, egalitarianism, multiculturalism, and equal outcomes. In chapter 9 we will delve further into politics, in which public education plays a key role.

In chapter 6 we will discuss the family, but it bears the remark that part of the design of public education is for the purpose of undermining the family. Through public schools, the state can be the mother and father of our children. Remember, they are to be socialized as much or more than they are to be educated. What is the point of education? It once was to teach our children how to think about God's world and what is required to live in it. Now it is not about that at all. Now it is about simultaneously learning self-expression and conformity to the group, primarily through play, group projects, and socializing. The progressive government has been clamoring for free, if not mandatory, nursery school from the womb. The earlier they can get them to the Tree of Knowledge the better.

But what is education meant for? Is there a way to learn, to be educated, to get knowledge without getting the "knowledge of good and evil" that kills? The answer is, that there must be, for humans are learning beings. God made us different from animals in that he gave us the capacity to conceptualize. If we are going to educate our children in a way that is godly, we must work within the boundaries of how God intended the human mind, made in the image of his, to work.

Consider first that a child is born with what a scholar would call *tabula rasa*. This means he is an empty slate, an empty mind. A baby looks at the world and sees objects and people. He experiences sensations: pain, pleasure, joy, sadness, hunger, fulness, dryness, and wetness. He experiences all the world has to offer him, but he makes no sense of it. It is chaos to him. God has built in him a capacity to get knowledge, meaning, he has the capacity to make connections between all these facts of reality that surround him. He has been made in the image of God to conceptualize. This means he can see water, feel wetness, and understand they are connected. He can see his mother, taste milk, and make the connection. On that topic, he can feel hungry, drink milk, and experience relief from that feeling. The concept of hunger arrives before he can name it, but eventually, thanks to humans who are further along, he can even name it. He is "hungry," and he wants the stuff that comes from his mother by God's design, "milk."

Few people stop to consider just how remarkable this is. A mind is built, and thinking capacity is strengthened. A child learns to sense objects with his eyes, ears, nose, mouth, and hands. He then learns to create abstractions in his mind. Meaning he learns to formulate. He learns how to group things together in kind. He learns that A is A, but B is not A. He learns about the laws of causality. He learns that if he does this, then he causes that. He learns until he *knows.*

Our current education system is now an institution where the child learns until he *believes.* Do you understand how different that it is? In Christianity, the obsession is with faith. God obviously calls us to faith, but it is not blind faith. In the Bible, Abraham is commended for his faith. Now how did this faith come about? God spoke to him. Abraham received the Word of God. He was commanded by God to go to Canaan, to the land of promise, and though he was old and his wife was old, he was commanded to have offspring that outnumbered the sand on the beach and the stars in the sky. And Abraham believed in God, *so he obeyed.* That obedience was considered *faith* by God, and it was reckoned to him as *righteousness,* the very condition God calls His children to.

But Abraham's faith was *knowing.* He knew because there was something concrete to know. It was God's voice, God's ways, and God's call. It was God's conditional promise—the same promise held out to Adam: Life or Death. It was the same promise that would be held out to the Israelites upon their rescue from Egypt. It was even the same promise held out to Pharaoh: "Obey me and let my people go, or deal with the angel of Death."

Faith in the Bible is not that hard, because it is obvious for all to see. Remember Romans 1: (?) "What can be known about God is plain" from the creation, so "they are without excuse." God's children are called to *know*. Biblical faith is actually biblical knowing.

This is crucially important because what we are told today is that faith is not knowing. We are called to faith in things that cannot be known. We are called to faith in the state, faith in socialism and communism, faith in the state education system, faith that social security will be there, faith that printing money with no gold standard will not lead to the collapse of the dollar, and of Western civilization. Faith that if we give our children to the state, they will not raise them to be disintegrated, woke, and confused victims who don't know a man from a woman, who don't know murder from women's rights (to choose), who don't know the children of light from the children of darkness, the people of God from the beasts who look like them.

The way faith is sold is similar to the way Hitler sold it to the Germans who did not know God and were starving for significance in a leader, a *Fuhrer*. The Nazis preached faith by saying something, and I'm paraphrasing, like "if you know you know; if you don't know, then you are incapable of knowing." They preached faith in the perfection of the *Fuhrer* with no proof whatsoever to back up their claims that he must be blindly obeyed. To not simply just know it, was to have no faith, to be an unbeliever. This knowing was the very opposite of the knowing that Abraham, who had encountered God, possessed.

Or consider the faith of communist Russia. "Have faith that these austerity measures will pay off eventually. Have faith that we won't even need a state once we have all been enlightened and raised our consciousness to a new level. Have faith that the 20 million who have starved or died in the gulags for the good of the collective will not have died in vain. Hold out starving for a little while longer. Have faith, or be killed. This is not the *knowing* of Abraham and the children of God.

This education system fails many children because they cannot and have not developed a taste for apples. The diet our schools are feeding the minds of our children is in opposition to the truth that is hardwired into their souls. "But the word **is** very nigh unto thee, **in thy** mouth, and **in thy heart**, that thou mayest do **it**" (Deut 30:14 KJV, emphasis added).

So then what is proper education? It is the learning of facts so that the child can conceptualize. He can take abstractions and turn them into concretes. And he can also take concretes and formulate abstractions, that is, concepts. He can become *wise,* and the Bible says, "In all your getting, get wisdom." Again, remember what it says in Romans 1:20,

> **For his invisible attributes, namely, his eternal power and divine nature, have been clearly perceived, ever since the creation of the world, in the things that have been made. (ESV)**

This is abstracting and conceptualizing at its finest! To "perceive" the creation, and formulate the concept of God is high-order thinking. Our schools should be helping with this. They should be teaching reality to our children so that our children can be wise and know God. But they cannot do that, because that is not what government-run schools were designed to do. Our children need this knowledge because of one thing, God has designed them to make choices, particularly the important choices: good over evil, obedience to God's laws or rebellion, Life or Death. Our schools only teach them various ways of choosing death—Death by faith.

What Can Be Done?

There are two possible remedies to this malady. One would be for those who *know* the truth to establish schools based on the learning of true facts—biblical facts, scientific facts, historical facts, mathematical facts, and philosophical facts. By philosophy, I don't mean the nonsense that is nothing but idiotic contradictions, such as, "how do we know we're really here?" That is satanic and it is designed to undercut truth and true knowledge. If that is any kind of knowledge at all, it is the forbidden knowledge of Good and Evil that is nonsensical to the children of God, but the intellectual stock and trade of the children of Satan.

The other way is for the children of God to take the education of their own children into their own hands. How to homeschool is beyond the scope of this book, but it should be carefully considered by godly parents. However, there are some principles to consider when setting up a homeschool. Even if you don't homeschool, these principles apply to parenting in general.

1. The primary purpose of education is learning to think independently. God has equipped each person with a mind as our main tool for living. Public education today is designed to teach children to let someone else, in general, the government, think for them. This is communism.

2. In this day of over-parenting, we must be careful not to protect our children from adversity and discomfort. Life comes with adversity and discomfort built in. The only way our children will grow up to be happy and successful adult children of God is if we teach them to face and overcome adversity, which is one of the keys to a life well lived.

3. Education is for teaching rational principles of thought (see #1), and *not*, as the education system today thinks, for socializing children. Why would we want other children or most left educators socializing our children? That is our job.

4. The Bible is the most crucial subject to study in homeschool, without a biblical foundation and worldview, the children of God will not be equipped to "subdue the earth" on behalf of God, who has given them the authority to do so.

5. After the Bible, the key subjects that must be learned are history, literature, science, math, and language arts. I myself was led back to the Bible and truth by the study of history and science. Nothing helps a child understand

the way men behave and the consequences of that behavior better than studying these things in the past. Literature shows the nature of man and a range of good and evil. Science, math, and language arts show the logic of the way God created the earth. The eloquence of 2 + 2 = 4 shows the balance of God's mind and the laws of logic and causality. If children learn these things, they will understand principles without even knowing they understand them. They will think logically, critically, and wisely.

God creates a child with certain genetic propensities, but he also creates them tabula rasa, a blank slate. We must carefully put in place the building blocks of *knowing.* The only thing that can lead to proper action is proper understanding.

Our schools have become broken. We cannot trust the state to educate our children. If you must have your kids in public school, then you must stay vigilant. Ask them what they are learning. Challenge the assumptions being made. Poke holes in the illogic, and guide them through it. They will survive, only if you don't fall asleep on the job.

Chapter 6

The Family Blood

"From Baby Boom to Baby Doom."

-James Dubose

"Two things your enemy doesn't want you to have is the truth and babies."

-James Dubose

By the end of my twelfth-grade year, my future wife would become pregnant with my first of seven sons. When she was two or three months pregnant, I departed for army basic training. What I did not know then was that the birth of my first son would determine who I would become.

The Devil, through one of his minions, advised my wife and me to abort our son. In the expert opinion of this man, the child she carried would have a difficult life, if he survived at all. We were told we'd spend our own pathetic lives caring for him as he would never be able to do anything for himself.

Maybe it was because of my youth, but I never really was worried about it, nor did I think much of it. I asked my wife how she felt about the possibility of raising a child with spina bifida. She said she felt fine, and that was all I needed to hear. I had peace. My wife was troubled by the "expert opinion," but she was willing to go forward. Nine months later she delivered a healthy 6 lb, 13 oz baby boy. It would not be the last time that doctors attempted to use fear to persuade us to do what they wanted us to do. I didn't know this then, but I do now: a person is the culmination of the choices they make. Period. The choices you make in life define who you are. It is never about what a person says, only about what he has done, does, and will do.

Remember in the last chapter we said this was supposed to be the point of our education as children. But the schools can't teach it. It is taught in the home.

Be Fruitful and Multiply

God's command was, "be fruitful and multiply" (Gen 1:28).

There is so much that obeying this command accomplishes. On the surface, it just seems elementary, but one of God's goals is to undermine Satanists. Big family has a direct relationship to freedom. Social security is not a check from the government. *Social security* is something that is provided by big families. It is big families that provide community stability and extended care for their elders and childcare. It is big families that police themselves and the community. Its children are the glue that makes a community. Most of the time it's the relationships that children form in the community with other children that gives adults a reason to know one another. Big families are the financial safety net that allows family members to lean upon one another during financial hardships.

How can you undermine this functioning social order? You have to diminish the family so that those things that we relied on each other for, we then become dependent upon the state to provide.

The more children you have, the more freedoms you have.

Consider the wealth that has been stolen from American citizens by the state. Social Security has collected trillions of dollars since its inception. Social Security is almost no different than annuities that are provided by insurance companies. The one difference, however, is that the agreement you have with the insurance company is binding. The state arbitrarily changes the rules based on whatever is best for the state and its ability to pay. Consider the wealth that is lost when an American dies before he collects SSI. If that same person had an annuity and he never collected, the money would go to his survivors. Instead, the state becomes the beneficiary, never having to return the principle or interest to surviving family members. My point is that the community does not need the state.

The created world belongs to God, and He gave it to his children to maintain. In order for Satan and his followers to steal what belongs to God and His children, he needs the authority of big government. Again, the purpose of the Bible is that God's children will know how to live freely.

The Devil is patient and God has an eternity.

There is a disconnection between the decisions we make now and how those decisions affect us in the future. The Bible gives us the insight we need in order to make the right decisions going forward. The little things that we dismiss as unimportant play a significant part in the way the world looks today. The devil uses subtle changes in order to bring about a great influence and change in culture later.

For instance, today it's not even a talking point to consider when you see a woman wearing pants. Yet, we had Hillary Clinton who ran for president, and that was a significant part of her attire. In the past, something as insignificant as the wearing of pants by women was seen as something liberating, and it was. Those subtle changes would later have your newly appointed Supreme Court Justice unable to answer a simple question, "What is a woman?"

She's a mother with two daughters and she betrayed her truth. That recording of her failure will be with her for the rest of her life. There's no gift greater you can give your children and future descendants than the truth.

Maybe some would consider that a stretch. Then how about the fact that there was a time when married men and women were never shown in bed on television? There was also a time before we saw the horrifying shower scene from Alfred Hitchcock's *Psycho*, where all you saw was the blood go down the drain. A woman brutally murdered on TV is the subtle cultural change needed to begin moving society towards death. Television of the past protected the minds of innocent children. There wasn't a TV world of over-sexualized men and women, heterosexual or otherwise and you didn't see children harmed and killed.

So what happened? American TV slowly introduced images of men and women in bed together. Then they gave us comedians in drag...and we laughed. While we were laughing, we non-verbally communicated to our children that the culture of men in dresses and women in pants is no big deal. What did we think would happen next?

The *knowledge* that man acquires allows him the ability to do things today that were science-fiction of the past. Every gift has a curse. Television can be used to report news, educate, and exchange ideas, but it can also be weaponized. For America today the weapon of mass destruction is the TV. There was a time when you only had to tell children that what is on TV isn't real. Now adult children do not know the difference either. The TV has become the mouthpiece of their new God. When this device tells you to stay away from friends and family or to accept a vaccine, you obey.

Your faith that requires trust is now influenced by what's suggested on TV. A trust and a faith that was reserved for your earthly mother and your Heavenly Father. Now we watch as millions of people line up so that their new parents can tell healthy people if they are sick and sick people if they are healthy. How did the state gain the trust of the people?

They liberated the mother and made it easy to destroy the traditional family of mother and father. Now the state has become the primary teacher of children, and once you become educated, you trust those who have given you the knowledge. They have taught you everything you know and have now transitioned you from distrust to trust. Your faith in God has been replaced by your trust in knowledge. You now have a new religion and new belief system. The Covid-19 vaccination was a display of trust in man, instead of faith in God.

> 15 **And the LORD will take away from thee all sickness, and
> will put none of the evil diseases of Egypt, which thou
> knowest, upon thee; but will lay them upon all them that hate
> thee. 16 And thou shalt consume all the people which the
> LORD thy God shall deliver thee; thine eye shall have no pity
> upon them: neither shalt thou serve their gods; for that will be
> a snare unto thee. (Deut 7:15-16 KJV)**

The founders of this nation understood that the state is not to be trusted and for this reason formed the Constitution for the laws of this land. The entire purpose of the Constitution is that men are not to trust the state, understanding that the nature of some men who have power is to want more power. The Constitution of The United States is simply an anti-communist document. Those who are in opposition to God's people will seek to take away your voice, that is why I mentioned earlier that it is a good reason why the Bible is written as a story.

The Amendments are solely meant to protect the people from the state. Once the people begin to trust the state, they are now moving away from God and towards Death. When the people begin to do this, the obvious result is that the laws of the state begin to tower over the laws of God.

> 49 **The LORD shall bring a nation against thee from far, from the end of the earth, as swift as the eagle flieth; a nation whose tongue thou shalt not understand;**

> 52 **And he shall besiege thee in all thy gates, until thy high and fenced walls come down, wherein thou trusted, throughout all thy land: and he shall besiege thee in all thy gates throughout all thy land, which the LORD thy God hath given thee. Deuteronomy 28:49,52 KJV**

Contrary to what many believe there really aren't any atheists. You may have those who do not accept Christian doctrine and so they consider themselves atheists. Or you may have those who do not believe there is a God at all, and for this reason, they call themselves atheists. The truth however is that if you don't have a God one will be appointed to you. This is what communism represents, it's about expanding the powers of the State and the State is now your God. You do not get to opt out. In a democratic society, you are given the freedom to be wrong about God, but over time, continued disobedience to the one true God will result in your forced obedience to the state.

If the wisdom to choose Life is learned in the home within the nuclear family as God designed it, the evil one's plan in league with the government cannot undermine the family. There are several sociological factors that have worked to accomplish this. They are:

- Feminism and Women's Lib
- The Welfare System
- Legalized Abortion
- No-Fault Divorce and Revisionist Views of Marriage
- Gay Marriage
- Communism and Groups Built on Marxist Ideology, Such as BLM
- Herding and Depopulating

Let us consider the first five of each of these in turn. The sixth, Communism, will be considered thoroughly in chapter 9.

Feminism

In an article on Feminism on the website for The History Channel, it is described as "a belief in the political, economic and cultural equality of women." (Citation) Who doesn't want women to have political, economic, and cultural equality? If women are being kept from these things by force, then we should stop at nothing to remedy that. They are made in the image of God with creative and reasoning capacity, and they should be free to live as such.

But that is not ever where the argument ends. It is only the beginning, and when you pull back the lid from Feminism, you find the same Serpent who was advocating for this doctrine back in Genesis3. Feminism is considered to have come in four waves in modern times.

First Wave Feminism

The first wave dealt with property rights, voting, and access to education. Though there had been feminists as far back as Ancient Greece and Rome, Abigail Adams, wife of John Adams, was an early advocate of modern first-wave feminism. Imagine the American people after they had fought for freedom, life, liberty, and the pursuit of happiness for all men because all men were created equal. The philosophical foundations were laid by the Founders, and the unrest was a matter of time.

Also adding to the conversation was the fact many of the leading abolitionists were women, and they were not oblivious to the fact that they were fighting for equality of a kind for black men that they themselves were not allowed. This could not last without backlash. When in the 19th century, Elizabeth Cady

Stanton, and Lucretia Mott advocated for "their sacred right to the elective franchise" at the 1848 Seneca Falls Convention, it was Frederick Douglass who spoke on their behalf, saying he could not accept the equal rights for blacks if they were not also given to women. By 1920, Susan B. Anthony led the charge and, because of women's participation in the efforts of the Great War, the 19th Amendment was passed, granting women the right to vote. Women also began to enter the workplace in greater numbers.

Second Wave Feminism

In the second wave, feminists began to lobby and protest for "women's liberation" from the "limited roles" of homemaking and child-rearing, because, according to one of their heroes, Betty Friedan, these were "boring" occupations. Congress passed a ban on sexual discrimination in 1972, and the crowing achievement in the eyes of second-wave feminists was the recently upended victory of Roe v. Wade and the right to kill their unborn babies if they didn't want them.

Third Wave Feminism

The third wave came about when critics of earlier movements began to point out that there had not been enough emphasis on the rights of women of color, lesbians, and women of religious minorities. This wave kicked off in 1991 when Anita Hill testified before an all-male congressional committee, and Clarence Thomas, who she had accused of sexual harassment, was confirmed to the Supreme Court. The third wave led to #me too and various other cultural phenomena like the rejection of the binary (male and female), which I have already stated as created by God and crucial to grasp if one wants to understand the nature of the world.

Fourth Wave Feminism

By 2012, the third wave had bled into the fourth wave of feminism. The fourth wave is characterized by the empowerment of women and the idea of intersectionality. Intersectionality has to do with the combination of a person's identities for which they are oppressed on some level. For instance, if you are a woman, you have a case to make that you are in the oppressed class. But if you are a black woman, you have a greater case. If you are a black woman who is part Mexican, you have a greater case, if you are also the single mom of a child with disabilities, congratulations, you are truly oppressed. Now add that you are a lesbian and the world is your oyster.

How does the enemy use feminism to undermine the biblical design? First, there is nothing that can be done to meet the demands of feminists that don't require some sort of collectivism. Because right away a woman must rely on her victimized group identity in order to elevate her importance. This group must then pressure whoever is in charge to *give* them what they want—their so-called "rights." But right there you have a contradiction. You can't use collectivism to grant individualistic rights. Rights by nature can only be individual.

The other more obvious way that feminism undermines biblical design is simple in that it elevates the roles of women in the workplace and polis, and denigrates the traditional roles of motherhood and homemaking, so that women who secretly desire that sort of life, purpose, and calling, feel ashamed and don't follow that path.

Similarly, the idea of a woman becoming a helpmeet for her husband is considered sacrilege in any wave of feminism. This biblical concept is that God creates a man and calls him to a purpose in the world. He sends him to go and "subdue the earth and rule over it." He brings to the man a woman "meet for him," (Gen 2), who the man recognizes as "bone of my bone and flesh of my flesh." She "helps" him in ways that only she can. He cares for her, provides for her, and protects her and their children, and she keeps his home and carries and nurtures his babies. If this sounds like a boring and one-dimensional life, it is far from it. A look at the biblical Proverbs 31 woman shows what God had in mind for a helpmeet.

> **10 Who can find a virtuous woman? for her price is far above rubies.**
>
> **11 The heart of her husband doth safely trust in her, so that he shall have no need of spoil.**
>
> **12 She will do him good and not evil all the days of her life.**
>
> **13 She seeketh wool, and flax, and worketh willingly with her hands.**
>
> **14 She is like the merchants' ships; she bringeth her food from afar.**
>
> **15 She riseth also while it is yet night, and giveth meat to her household, and a portion to her maidens.**

16 She considereth a field, and buyeth it: with the fruit of her
hands she planteth a vineyard.

17 She girdeth her loins with strength, and strengtheneth her
arms.

18 She perceiveth that her merchandise is good: her candle
goeth not out by night.

19 She layeth her hands to the spindle, and her hands hold the
distaff.

20 She stretcheth out her hand to the poor; yea, she reacheth
forth her hands to the needy.

21 She is not afraid of the snow for her household: for all her
household are clothed with scarlet.

22 She maketh herself coverings of tapestry; her clothing is silk
and purple.

23 Her husband is known in the gates, when he sitteth among
the elders of the land.

24 She maketh fine linen, and selleth it; and delivereth girdles
unto the merchant.

25 Strength and honour are her clothing; and she shall rejoice
in time to come.

26 She openeth her mouth with wisdom; and in her tongue is
the law of kindness.

[27] She looketh well to the ways of her household, and eateth not the bread of idleness.

[28] Her children arise up, and call her blessed; her husband also, and he praiseth her.

[29] Many daughters have done virtuously, but thou excellest them all.

[30] Favour is deceitful, and beauty is vain: but a woman that feareth the Lord, she shall be praised.

[31] Give her of the fruit of her hands; and let her own works praise her in the gates. (Prov 31:10-31)

It sounds like this woman is busy helping her husband to be respected at the gates of the city because of his good and capable wife. She herself is respected and blessed. This is the standard of God's design, and it is fulfilling and a part of the abundant life for a woman. A brief glance through the verses is helpful.

Verse 10: She is praised for her character, her virtue. For men and women alike, what matters is their character. For men and women alike, the standard is godliness, and we have our best life when we, the children of God conform to his image.

Verse 11: She is a delight to her husband, again, because of her virtue. And because of her, he doesn't lack material possessions.

Verse 12: She does her husband good.

Verse 13: She is skilled at producing the things her family needs.

Verse 14: She is a person of abundance. She makes sure her family is fed.

Verse 15: She is not lazy, and she may well oversee some employees (maidens) in the household.

Verse 16: She makes herself wise in business, especially concerning things that benefit her family.

Verse 17: She takes care of her physical health.

Verse 18: She buys quality goods for her family.

Verse 19: She is not idle, but works hard.

Verse 20: She has a generous heart.

Verse 21: She is prepared for the seasons.

Verse 22: She sees that her family is dressed according to their prosperity.

Verse 23: She minds her husband's reputation.

Verse 24: She has a good head for business and contributes financially to the family if necessary.

Verse 25: She is an honorable woman with strong character. This will lead to good times.

Verse 26: She's not a gossip or a nag. When she speaks, it is to convey wisdom and kind words. She is gracious and wise.

Verse 27: She manages her home: children, servants, and is always working.

Verse 28: Her family sees her worth, and considers her blessed by God to be such a good woman.

Verse 29: Again, she is virtuous.

Verse 30: Her reverence for God underlies all of the above activities.

Verse 31: She should be rewarded for her virtuous actions.

Feminists should see that everything they hope for is on this list. Rather than being a feminist, the women of God must seek to be godly. All the worth in the universe is in this endeavor. While the feminists are marching and protesting, the Proverbs 31 woman is living her life to the fullest, receiving the fruit of her labor, and hearing her husband and children rise up and call her blessed. She is building a home for her family, and even making money. She doesn't stress about the pay gap, or whether the world values her. She values herself and what she can accomplish. She takes the cultural mandate to image-bearers and runs with it, pursuing an abundant life in God. While the feminist turns uglier and angrier by the minute, the biblical woman flourishes and becomes more radiant every day.

All these ills are related to the way Satan is attacking this world. The Five Deadly Axioms Of A Superior Enemy are: Depopulate, Emasculate, Demilitarize, Demonetize, and Demoralize. Feminism accomplishes at least four of these.

The serpent offered Eve an apple from the tree of knowledge, which is actually the tree of death and she did eat.

Today that Apple is called Women's Lib. The serpent offered Eve what the modern woman is being offered today...liberation. What truly is women's lib? Liberation from her man, her child, and her God.

The first feminist was the serpent. This is one of the lessons the story of Adam and Eve is trying to teach, this is what the story is trying to warn us about.

My short narrative of the story of Adam and Eve is:

When weak men follow disobedient women, that is the beginning of the destruction of God's children. After Adam and Eve disobeyed, this would be the last conversation they would have with God. Man would not hear the voice of God again until the birth of Adam's grandson, Enoch.

Special people must do special things. Common people... that's the life Adam and Eve chose.

A Word About Women Pastors

There is one other phenomenon that must be understood regarding the roles of men and women in the Church. There is no question that God created men and women to be equal in dignity. Both men and women have the opportunity to earn the respect of others through their choices, which are a product of their character. Both have the opportunity to lose respect. Both are image bearers of God (Gen 1:28), and both have a choice to Live or Die, to obey God or disobey God.

But men and women are not the same. They are different. They are made differently for different roles, and I've written about this already. We can debate all day about the phenomenon of women leading men in the workplace. Even those of us who acknowledge that men and women are made differently for different things will debate that. Bible verses can be used by both sides of that debate (although one side must take them out of context). But what is clear from Scripture is that there is one role forbidden to women in the Church. That is the role of Pastor/Elder/Overseer.

Here are some of the New Testament verses on the topic:

> **"I do not permit a woman to teach or to exercise authority over a man; rather, she is to remain quiet" (1 Tim 2:12 ESV).**

"Let a woman learn quietly with all submissiveness. I do not permit a woman to teach or to exercise authority over a man; rather, she is to remain quiet. For Adam was formed first, then Eve; and Adam was not deceived, but the woman was deceived and became a transgressor. Yet she will be saved through childbearing—if they continue in faith and love and holiness, with self-control" (1 Tim 2:11-15 ESV).

> **"The women should keep silent in the churches. For they are not permitted to speak, but should be in submission, as the Law also says" (1 Cor 4:34 ESV).**

And when the description is given of the qualifications of an elder, it says,

> **The saying is trustworthy: If anyone aspires to the office of overseer, he desires a noble task. Therefore an overseer must be above reproach, the husband of one wife, sober-minded, self-controlled, respectable, hospitable, able to teach, not a drunkard, not violent but gentle, not quarrelsome, not a lover of money. He must manage his own household well, with all**

> **dignity keeping his children submissive, for if someone does not know how to manage his own household, how will he care for God's church? (1 Tim 1:3-7 ESV).**

Today, many groups have worked around these verses in order to keep up with the times. This is called egalitarianism. In the strictest sense of the word, egalitarianism refers to the idea that "all people are equal and deserve equal opportunities." What could be wrong with that? Only people have expanded the definition to mean "all people deserve equal *outcomes*." I will discuss the satanic nature of this doctrine later. But Christian Feminists have adopted the word to mean that women should be allowed to be pastors.

What they use for this doctrine is something called a Trajectory Hermeneutic. *Hermeneutic* refers to one's method of reading the Bible, of interpretation. The *Trajectory Hermeneutic* says that the Bible shows a trajectory of greater and greater freedoms for all people and especially for women. The theory goes that if only the Bible had kept going, it would have continued to liberate women all the way to free them up to be pastors (and heads of their families). The Bible, they say, was written in a time when the peoples of the world just couldn't get there, because they were so much more backward than us enlightened modern people. They do God a big favor by letting us know what God was going to say next.

Only he didn't. In fact, the last verses of the Bible give a stern warning to anyone who would presume to know how to add to Scripture:

> **[18] For I testify unto every man that heareth the words of the prophecy of this book, If any man shall add unto these things, God shall add unto him the plagues that are written in this book:**
>
> **[19] And if any man shall take away from the words of the book of this prophecy, God shall take away his part out of the book of life, and out of the holy city, and from the things which are written in this book. (Rev 22:18-19 KJV)**

What's wrong with the trajectory hermeneutic? Imagine what doors are opened by this interpretation. All one has to do is imagine what God might have eventually said based on the way they interpret the Bible to be going. Did you know that the 1940s and 50s were when the first denominations to debate ordaining women pastors started their debates? Did you know that every single one of these denominations is now debating, or past debating the ordination of gay pastors and the marital union of homosexuals? If our doctrine expands to include whatever we predict "God might have said eventually," then what would be off limits? Clear Scripture to the contrary in the known Canon is not enough to refute what God "might have said eventually."

But we have gotten away from the topic of family. What else has the evil one used to undermine the biblical family unit?

The Welfare System

A reading of the Old Testament confirms without a doubt that God loves for his children to care for the poor. Allow me to overwhelm you with evidence.

> **Proverbs 19:17 ESV Whoever is generous to the poor lends to the Lord, and he will repay him for his deed.**
>
> **Proverbs 14:31 ESV Whoever oppresses a poor man insults his Maker, but he who is generous to the needy honors him.**
>
> **Proverbs 22:9 ESV Whoever has a bountiful eye will be blessed, for he shares his bread with the poor.**
>
> **1 John 3:17-18 ESV But if anyone has the world's goods and sees his brother in need, yet closes his heart against him, how does God's love abide in him? Little children, let us not love in word or talk but in deed and in truth.**
>
> **Proverbs 28:27 ESV Whoever gives to the poor will not want, but he who hides his eyes will get many a curse.**
>
> **Deuteronomy 15:11 ESV For there will never cease to be poor in the land. Therefore I command you, 'You shall open wide your hand to your brother, to the needy and to the poor, in your land.'**
>
> **Galatians 2:10 ESV Only, they asked us to remember the poor, the very thing I was eager to do.**
>
> **Proverbs 21:13 ESV Whoever closes his ear to the cry of the poor will himself call out and not be answered.**

Proverbs 14:21 ESV Whoever despises his neighbor is a sinner, but blessed is he who is generous to the poor.

Deuteronomy 15:10-11 ESV You shall give to him freely, and your heart shall not be grudging when you give to him, because for this the Lord your God will bless you in all your work and in all that you undertake. For there will never cease to be poor in the land. Therefore I command you, 'You shall open wide your hand to your brother, to the needy and to the poor, in your land.'

1 John 3:17 ESV But if anyone has the world's goods and sees his brother in need, yet closes his heart against him, how does God's love abide in him?

Proverbs 29:7 ESV A righteous man knows the rights of the poor; a wicked man does not understand such knowledge.

Deuteronomy 15:7-8 ESV "If among you, one of your brothers should become poor, in any of your towns within your land that the Lord your God is giving you, you shall not harden your heart or shut your hand against your poor brother, but you shall open your hand to him and lend him sufficient for his need, whatever it may be.

Ezekiel 16:49 ESV Behold, this was the guilt of your sister Sodom: she and her daughters had pride, excess of food, and prosperous ease, but did not aid the poor and needy.

Leviticus 19:15 ESV "You shall do no injustice in court. You shall not be partial to the poor or defer to the great, but in righteousness shall you judge your neighbor.

Leviticus 25:35 ESV "If your brother becomes poor and cannot maintain himself with you, you shall support him as though he were a stranger and a sojourner, and he shall live with you.

Deuteronomy 15:10 ESV You shall give to him freely, and your heart shall not be grudging when you give to him, because for this the Lord your God will bless you in all your work and in all that you undertake.

Isaiah 58:6-7 ESV "Is not this the fast that I choose: to loose the bonds of wickedness, to undo the straps of the yoke, to let the oppressed go free, and to break every yoke? Is it not to share your bread with the hungry and bring the homeless poor into your house; when you see the naked, to cover him, and not to hide yourself from your own flesh?

Proverbs 17:5 ESV Whoever mocks the poor insults his Maker; he who is glad at calamity will not go unpunished.

Isaiah 61:1 ESV The Spirit of the Lord God is upon me, because the Lord has anointed me to bring good news to the poor; he has sent me to bind up the brokenhearted, to proclaim liberty to the captives, and the opening of the prison to those who are bound;

Leviticus 19:9-10 ESV "When you reap the harvest of your land, you shall not reap your field right up to its edge, neither shall you gather the gleanings after your harvest. And you shall not strip your vineyard bare, neither shall you gather the fallen grapes of your vineyard. You shall leave them for the poor and for the sojourner: I am the Lord your God.

Jeremiah 22:16 ESV He judged the cause of the poor and needy; then it was well. Is not this to know me? declares the Lord.

Psalm 82:3-4 ESV Give justice to the weak and the fatherless; maintain the right of the afflicted and the destitute. Rescue the weak and the needy; deliver them from the hand of the wicked."

Deuteronomy 15:7 ESV "If among you, one of your brothers should become poor, in any of your towns within your land that the Lord your God is giving you, you shall not harden your heart or shut your hand against your poor brother,

Isaiah 1:17 ESV Learn to do good; seek justice, correct oppression; bring justice to the fatherless, plead the widow's cause.

Isaiah 41:17 ESV When the poor and needy seek water, and there is none, and their tongue is parched with thirst, I the Lord will answer them; I the God of Israel will not forsake them.

Psalm 35:10 ESV All my bones shall say, "O Lord, who is like you, delivering the poor from him who is too strong for him, the poor and needy from him who robs him?"

Proverbs 22:16 ESV Whoever oppresses the poor to increase his own wealth, or gives to the rich, will only come to poverty.

Psalm 12:5 ESV "Because the poor are plundered, because the needy groan, I will now arise," says the Lord; "I will place him in the safety for which he longs."

> **Ezekiel 22:29 ESV The people of the land have practiced extortion and committed robbery. They have oppressed the poor and needy, and have extorted from the sojourner without justice.**

> **Deuteronomy 15:7-11 ESV "If among you, one of your brothers should become poor, in any of your towns within your land that the Lord your God is giving you, you shall not harden your heart or shut your hand against your poor brother, but you shall open your hand to him and lend him sufficient for his need, whatever it may be. Take care lest there be an unworthy thought in your heart and you say, 'The seventh year, the year of release is near,' and your eye look grudgingly on your poor brother, and you give him nothing, and he cry to the Lord against you, and you be guilty of sin. You shall give to him freely, and your heart shall not be grudging when you give to him, because for this the Lord your God will bless you in all your work and in all that you undertake. For there will never cease to be poor in the land. Therefore I command you, 'You shall open wide your hand to your brother, to the needy and to the poor, in your land.'**

These verses and many others leave no doubt that God wants us to care for those in need. One massive problem in the ancient world, which is still a problem today, is the propensity to treat the poor unjustly—that is, to take advantage of the poor. God will judge harshly those who commit such an injustice. God also wants his people to be generous with the poor.

But does that mean the non-theocratic government should take from some (by force) to support others? In a representative government like the United States, there is no biblical warrant for a group of elites, elected or otherwise, to decide to use their monopoly on the use of force, to take (at gunpoint and the threat of prison) the money of one man to give to another. God may call us to be generous, but how is it generous to have someone steal our money to give to someone else?

The World Produces Abundance

Many people look around the world today and see that some are rich and others are poor. They see that some are well-fed, and others starve. They shake their fist at God, nature, and reality. They clamor for solutions. They run to the "educated," and they yield themselves to "philosopher kings" who know better than them. They beg them to rule over them and take good care of them. They demand a politician to fix the "problems of the world."

But God's created world produces an abundance—there are no shortages. *Shortages are created by those in opposition to God.* If God's people win, the world wins. If God's people lose the battle, failing to steward the world as mandated at Adam's creation, then evil wins, destruction wins, scarcity wins, fear, pain, and suffering win. The darkness wins. If we can recapture the vision laid out in Genesis 1:26-28, then we can recapture the world.

> **26 Then God said, "Let us make man in our image, after our likeness. And let them have dominion over the fish of the sea and over the birds of the heavens and over the livestock and over all the earth and over every creeping thing that creeps on the earth."**

The Deserving Poor

It is worth talking about the idea that a man's need is not the main criteria to consider when it comes to supporting his material needs. In 2 Thessalonians 3:10, it says, "For even when we were with you, this we commanded you, that if any would not work, neither should he eat." In the days the Bible was written, there was a much greater likelihood that a man could find himself destitute by the injustice of another. The rule of law that we still *basically* live by in America is a relatively new phenomenon that we absolutely take for granted. We are not perfect, but we have so many more freedoms, so far than the vast majority of the world.

This creates confusion when it comes to answering the question of how to care for the poor among us. Is there a difference between he who is poor by oppression and he who is poor by his own laziness, or worse, his lack of integrity, industry, or consciousness? I think there is a difference. We will talk later about the horrors of abortion, but the debate around it features is one of the reasons for this confusion. Pro-Choice advocates claim that this issue is a human rights issue—what is at stake being a "woman's right to choose."

They are correct that it is a human rights issue. They are incorrect concerning who the victim is. There is one who has all the power, and that is the woman. There is one who has no power, that is the baby in the womb. This is what we mean by "the deserving poor." A society that enables the undeserving poor, that is, those who have made themselves destitute by their choices, will create greater and greater numbers of citizens prone to those same bad choices. But a society that has compassion for those who by no fault of their own have fallen on hard times will support its citizens well, and also foster a spirit of production.

Is this to say that such a society is not compassionate toward what we are calling the undeserving poor? Not at all. On the contrary, it is most compassionate to refuse to finance and reward bad behavior. Once we create a world in which choices don't really matter, we are doomed and so are those who live in such a world. In the abortion example, the vast majority of the time, the pregnant woman got that way by the choice she made, the endangered baby in the womb was not given a choice. It is the baby who must be prioritized in that situation.

This is exactly how God treats us. In spite of the way the gospel of Jesus Christ is falsely preached today—that is—the Savior who came to save our sorry souls since everyone is equally evil and equally unable to live as God desires—God actually expects us to keep to his ways if we would Live. God rewards those who follow him. Trusting in God is synonymous with trusting in his ways. Trusting in his ways is obeying him. If one is not obedient to God, then one betrays that he does not, in fact, trust God. Such was the case with Adam and Eve.

Though God continues to provide for sinners for a time, God compassionately refuses to reward and finance their bad behavior. He will watch his creation go to hell if that is what they choose. Make no mistake, he watches with compassion and lament, but he allows it because for us to be made in his image *requires* that we have free will to make our choices. He always holds out choices, and every choice he gives always amounts to the ultimate choice between Life and Death.

God's children are called to be compassionate and to be generous to the deserving poor, even kind but firm with the undeserving poor. In both cases, we are treating the person with dignity as a creation of God. Our welfare system seems designed by Satan to bring our country to its knees. There are some interesting statistics from the last fifty years that proves this.

The Institute for Family Studies points out that in 1960, only 9% of children in America were raised in a home without their father. Today, the number is 25%, and it is much higher for black families. What changed?

> From 1890 to 1950, black women had a higher marriage rate than white women. And in 1950, just 9% of black children lived without their fathers. By 1960, the black marriage rate had declined but remained close to the white marriage rate. In other words, despite open racism and widespread poverty, strong black families used to be the norm.
>
> But by the mid-1980s, black fatherlessness skyrocketed. Today, only 44% of black children have a father in the home. In unison, the rate of black out-of-wedlock births went from 24.5% in 1964 to 70.7% by 1994, roughly where it stands today.
>
> One contributor to family breakdown, which soon spread to the poor and working-class white families, may have been welfare expansion. Cash welfare in meager form existed since 1935, and some welfare expansion took place during the Kennedy administration. But under Johnson's Great Society, which began in 1964, benefits became

substantially more generous and came under greater control of the federal government.

In the words of Harvard's Paul Peterson, "some programs actively discouraged marriage," because "welfare assistance went to mothers so long as no male was boarding in the household… Marriage to an employed male, even one earning the minimum wage, placed at risk a mother's economic well-being." Infamous "man in the house" rules meant that welfare workers would randomly appear in homes to check and see if the mother was accurately reporting her family status.

The benefits available were extremely generous. According to Peterson, it was "estimated that in 1975 a household head would have to earn $20,000 a year to have more resources than what could be obtained from Great Society programs." In today's dollars, that's over $90,000 per year in earnings.

That may be a reason why, in 1964, only 7% of American children were born out of wedlock, compared to 40% today. As Jason Riley has noted, "the government paid mothers to keep fathers out of the home—and paid them well."

Assuming that the progressives truly had the best intentions, it shows the ineptitude of central planning. But even where progressives had good intentions, they played right into the hands of Satan, whose intentions are well known, "to steal and kill and destroy" (John 10:10). Division is a mark of the beast, the apple was offered and we ate.

Justice and Mercy are they Not the Same Thing

Nowadays, the Church is largely on board with the politicians. Even the conservatives have fallen in line with "helping the poor." Hardly anyone has the moral courage to denounce these destructive policies. In the Church, the cry is for "social justice." But what is social justice? Is social justice *justice*? If so, why does it need the modifier, "social"?

The Bible gives us the definition of justice.

> **[8] For I the Lord love justice; I hate robbery and wrong; I will faithfully give them their recompense, and I will make an everlasting covenant with them. (Isa 61:8 ESV)**

There are many verses that show God loves justice. But this verse gives a glimpse of the definition of justice. "I hate robbery." Robbery is unjust. So taking from others what belongs to them is unjust. Why? Consider the Ten Commandments: Two of the most foundational laws of God are "Thou shalt, not murder" and "Thou shalt not steal." God values Life. Throughout this entire book, I have shown this to be the case. So it is not hard to understand the commandment against murder.

But what are we to make of the commandment against theft? When one looks at history, it seems the world runs on theft. The strong take from the weak until someone stronger comes along to take from them, be it land, possessions, or women. But this is not God's way. Someone's possessions are a part of their life. To take something that someone else owns for the furthering of their life and that of their family is similar to murder and therefore unjust. Property rights are sacred to God, and it is miraculous that the Founders codified this in the Constitution.

So robbing someone is "wrong" and God hates it because he hates injustice. He hates injustice because he is perfectly just. He is righteous and loves righteousness.

He then says, "I will faithfully give them their recompense." *Recompense* is compensation for a wrong done. God is saying that he will make things right for those who have been treated unjustly. This itself is justice—doing what is right, giving people what they deserve. He will punish the wicked, and he will pay back the victims. This is the very definition of biblical justice.

Today, however, the word is used in place of the word "mercy." Mercy is shown when someone gets a benefit that they do not necessarily deserve. To give something that was not earned is mercy. God does love mercy. He says so in Lamentations 3:22, "It is of the Lord's mercies that we are not consumed because his compassions fail not." This is striking. The prophet is showing that in this case, God's mercy overcomes his justice. Instead of getting what we deserve, he is being patient and showing us mercy. And God does want us to show mercy as well.

If Christians understood this properly then they would see Jesus not only as the mercy of God (which they do), but also as an opportunity to return to the Father, to the fear of God, and to the Bible and the laws of God.

Social "Justice"

But the point is that mercy is mercy and justice is justice. Today, social justice is the phrase used to describe mercy. "They," say that it is justice to help the poor. It is justice if the poor were made poor by injustice. But if the poor were made poor by their choices, then helping them is mercy. That is, it is mercy if the help is not the toxic kind of help that keeps them poor. If we help in such a way that enables laziness or rewards them for not seeing themselves properly as image bearers of God who are called to find work to do, then our help is not merciful and it is not just.

When social justice is the kind of reparations that are being called for by the left, it is not justice and it is not mercy. It is, again, enabling. Not only that, reparations for slavery require that we squeeze people who were not alive in the days of slavery to pay up for those who were. It also assumes that there is anyone on the planet who did not descend from slaves in some culture at some point in time. Slavery was always a fact of existence on earth in every culture. Who then should get reparations?

True reparations come from God, not man. The mistake God's people continue to make is to ask man, for those things that God can and will give to you. If reparations are to be given by man, they'll come in the form of fiat currency. The reparations from God are the 'promised land,' your own nation. What good is money in an environment of oppression, where the state or your enemy owns the labor, the production, and the land? The end result will be that you'll render to Ceasar what belongs to Ceasar, Luke 20:25.

Exodus 6:2,4,7-8 KJV

> **And God spake unto Moses, and said unto him, I am the LORD: [4] And I have also established my covenant with them, to give them the land of Canaan, the land of their pilgrimage, wherein they were strangers. [7] And I will take you to me for a people, and I will be to you a God: and ye shall know that I am the LORD your God, which bringeth you out from under the burdens of the Egyptians. [8] And I will bring you in unto the land, concerning the which I did swear to give it to Abraham, to Isaac, and to Jacob; and I will give it to you for an heritage: I am the LORD.**

Mercy is mercy, and justice is justice. God does care about the poor, and he despises injustice, but it is the enemy's plan to conflate the two, confusing God's people who may mean well, and destroying the world in the process by rewarding the opposite behavior of what is required to thrive.

Legalized Abortion

In the above section, we began to consider abortion. In the very recent weeks as of this writing, the Supreme Court overturned the landmark decision in Roe v. Wade, saying that it was not the business of the Federal Supreme Court to decide such things and that those kinds of decisions should be legislative decisions at the state level. This was a great day for the Pro-Life cause, but it was also sadly off the mark of what could be done.

What good is the Supreme Court if it cannot rule against the murder of a child? Why would the states get to decide when it is okay to murder? The right to life is a fundamental axiomatic law. In fact, it is *the* fundamental law. "Thou shalt not murder." All our other laws are based on this one.

> **Psalm 139:13-16 ESV / For you formed my inward parts; you knitted me together in my mother's womb. I praise you, for I am fearfully and wonderfully made. Wonderful are your works; my soul knows it very well. My frame was not hidden from you, when I was being made in secret, intricately woven in the depths of the earth. Your eyes saw my unformed substance; in your book were written, every one of them, the days that were formed for me, when as yet there was none of them.**
>
> **Deuteronomy 30:19 ESV I call heaven and earth to witness against you today, that I have set before you life and death, blessing and curse. Therefore choose life, that you and your offspring may live**
>
> **Ecclesiastes 11:5 ESV As you do not know the way the spirit comes to the bones in the womb of a woman with child, so you do not know the work of God who makes everything.**
>
> **Psalm 127:3-5 ESV Behold, children are a heritage from the Lord, the fruit of the womb a reward. Like arrows in the hand of a warrior are the children of one's youth. Blessed is the man who fills his quiver with them! He shall not be put to shame when he speaks with his enemies in the gate.**

A society that tolerates legalized abortion in any of its states, is moving toward, rather than away from collapse. You don't make a policy of killing citizens without losing your society. No citizens, no country.

The Bible refers to God's people as children over 1000 times in the Bible. Of course one of the obvious definitions of a "child" is a young person, but another meaning given is someone who is strongly influenced by others. I'd like to suggest another definition, and that would be someone who doesn't know what happens next, which is to say that as it pertains to God, we are all children regardless of age. At 100 years of age, if you do not know what happens next, biblically you're a child.

Children need guidance from their parents because often they simply can not or do not reason the results of their decisions or actions. This is the current condition of America, and moreover, the world. America's condition is simply the result of God's children not understanding or asking the question, "What comes next?"

As children, it is not necessary to understand why. What is important is knowing that you must obey. Wisdom is important for knowing what is to be done and what will be the consequences if you don't do it. This is how the OT speaks to God's children, and this is how we parent our own children. The younger the child, the less conversation as to "why" they should obey. This is the normal progression of parent-child relationships. We do not get into lengthy discussions with our small children about not touching a hot stove. We give the order, and of course, they touch the hot stove anyway, and now they understand why they should have listened.

In the story of Adam and Eve, the hot stove is the Tree of the Knowledge of Good and Evil. The instructions were simple, as they typically are when instructing children. It is only after they disobeyed did they understand the severity of their actions. As our children mature, the threats are greater and more complex. They graduate to a point that someday they'll be required to protect and instruct their children. If we as parents fail to establish an authority for our children which is greater than we are, an authority that determines what is right and what is wrong, they will grow up believing they can decide for themselves their truth. This is reflected in the modern world. Man is now his authority as to who is God and what is right, simply because we do not know what comes next. Of all the lessons parents must teach their children between birth and adulthood, the most important is that there is an ultimate, Divine Authority. Obedience to parents was merely a stepping stone to obedience to God.

Previously, I described how God is in all things, and that matter and anti-matter can't coexist in the same space at the same time. God's children are behaving in a way that they are unaware of. Life on earth as children of God does not require psychic ability, only understanding. God's children aren't in need of a prophet, they need a teacher. There are many opinions, but only one truth, the goal of which is to understand life, death, freedom, and slavery, and the eternal impact of the decisions we make.

Hosea 4:6 says,

> **My people are destroyed for lack of knowledge: because thou hast rejected knowledge, I will also reject thee, that thou shalt be no priest to me: seeing thou hast forgotten the law of thy God, I will also forget thy children. (KJV)**

What comes next when we remove God from our currency? What comes next when we remove God from our schools and God from media and entertainment? What happens next when you remove God from the family, community, and nation?

These decisions lead to the current environment that exists in America which is hostile to children. The family, nation, and community have a responsibility to protect all children, those who are with us, and those who are yet born. Today we see children protesting for the right to abort because they do not know what's going to happen next. What happens next is an inability to secure the current freedoms that we have been granted.

The ridiculous argument that abolishing abortion takes away your freedom is false. It's actually the opposite that is true. The freedoms you have must be protected because your children are your future soldiers. It is your enemy who would rather want you to abort one million children rather than to face ten million on the battlefield. A reduction in population makes a nation vulnerable to attack and it is weakness that invites hostility. What follows pro-choice is *no-choice.* No-choice is not your ability to decide if you're pro-life or pro-choice, no, it's your inability to make any decisions at all. This is what bolshevism/ communism looks like. This is the condition in which billions of people around the world currently live.

Beholden To Our Families

A man is responsible for his family first and foremost. In communist countries, the family is undermined and denigrated. Black Lives Matter, an openly Marxist organization that doesn't care for any life, let alone black ones, originally publicized their whole mission but has recently hidden part of it due to obvious backlash. Before they removed it, their website stated,

> We disrupt the Western-prescribed nuclear family structure requirement by supporting each other as extended families and 'villages' that collectively care for one another.

Why? Because they correctly surmise that the family is a crucial part of a whole and healthy society. They know that if children are raised by their loving parents, the state will have a much more difficult time gaining absolute control over the child. They also know that if the family is undermined, the population of children will plummet. And when that happens, the end is near. Each man is responsible to care for and raise his family, to raise them in a community and nation where he must seek to maintain God's law at every level, starting with himself, then working outward to his family, his community, his state, his country, and finally, his world. Satanism and the collapse of the family and the world are allowed by the inaction of the godly. Only the action of the godly can stop its spread.

The Rapture

Christians debate the nature of the "rapture." The main debate focuses on the belief that Christians will be disappeared into heaven all at once as part of the events of the end times and the return of Christ. The main two viewpoints are that the rapture will either happen before the tribulation of seven years, or it will happen after it as Jesus returns. Both of these are wrong, the rapture is happening already. The U.S. population has already shrunk rapidly. By my estimation, half the population is gone. The world's population is collapsing and if you have been watching the news, you can see where this could be a driver of the things being obsessed over in the media.

What's so wrong and evil about this? The most obvious answer is that it is contrary to God's original law to man to "produce," and to "be fruitful and multiply" (Gen 1:28).

Abortion and Communism

Legalized abortion is a tool used by those who seek to transit us from democracy to communism. A small population is easier to control. The small population of children that currently exist is being indoctrinated in our schools and by our media into the idea of socialism.

> *"Give me four years to teach the children and the seed I have sown will never be uprooted."*
>
> — **Vladimir Ilyich Lenin**

What we have is an American society that doesn't value children. We simply do not understand what God and the enemy understand about the value of children. You're not only supposed to have them in abundance—"be fruitful and multiply"—but you're to protect them physically, emotionally, and mentally. This requires strong families and communities that represent God's values.

Socialist education (see chapter 5) produces children that are in opposition to God and family. Socialists promote abortion and homosexuality because big families and big government can't exist in the same place at the same time. One must annihilate the other, remember China's one-child policy. Big families and strong families do not need big government. Big families and strong communities earlier in America's history provided education and healthcare through philanthropy.

Welfare has not always been part of American policy and when initiated it required women not to have men in their homes.

These policies along with the promotion of feminism are the beginning of the destruction of the family. In *The Art of War*, "the goal is to destroy your enemy without ever firing a shot." Remember China's one-child policy, the destruction of family leads to the destruction of the community and the eventual fall of the nation, and the removal of personal freedoms. Feminism and women's lib accomplished what it was meant to accomplish, which is to separate the woman from her man, her children, and her God.

Children are the most vulnerable in a society in absence of the traditional family structure. The enemy is free to indoctrinate them with the verious ideas that oppose maintaining a democratic state. Welfare programs aided in removing the father from the home, and feminism promoted the idea of independent women. Independence removed women from the home and allowed the state to become the primary teacher of values. These children are the future Americans who'll rule over you. "As for my people, children are their oppressors, and women rule over them. O my people, they which lead thee cause thee to err, and destroy the way of thy paths" (Isa 3:12 KJV).

The children Isaiah 3:12 is referring to are those who do not know what will happen next. These are today's leaders. The enemy of free people today is the state. Parents are spending tens of thousands of dollars to send their children off to college only to return as pro-choice socialists.

We said that the root of this is feminism and the independent woman. Let's be clear. God created women to be *independent* in that they are not created to be mindless drones. Anyone not allowed to think for themselves and hold personal convictions is not a human, an image bearer of the Creator. That said, we are all created for community. When independent people who take responsibility for their ideas and thoughts join together in a "wise crowd" (rather than a herd, mob, or gang all beholden to a leader or mass hysteria), they form powerful communities. The most basic of these is a family. God created us to be independent, but He did not create us to be alone.

When one speaks now of the "independent" woman he is hardly speaking of a woman with her own mind. She is entirely dependent on the "knowledge of good and evil" that has been fed to her by the government, the schools, the culture, public opinion, the media, and Satan. But she is independent of family, of husband, or even her unborn child.

Communists have stated that the transition into communism is first accomplished by transitioning into socialism. It appears they may have not included a step, before we have socialism we have an *idiocracy*. No one in leadership appears to have any idea what will happen next. Where are America's Generals on the effects of family destruction and the abortion of their future soldiers? What are the economists' views on abortion and population reduction? America's economy is failing because the population has collapsed. America's churches are closing, because they didn't emphasize the first orders of the Creator, 'be fruitful and multiply". The condition of a nation is directly tied to the understanding of its leadership and our freedoms are directly associated with our ability to protect our children.

How can people defend themselves against their enemies if they abort their warriors in the womb? To all women who are with a child, you are not simply giving birth to a baby. You are giving birth to a future of millions, to an empire, and to a thriving civilization.

> **[15] And God said unto Abraham, As for Sarai thy wife, thou shalt not call her name Sarai, but Sarah shall her name be. [16] And I will bless her, and give thee a son also of her: yea, I will bless her, and she shall be a mother of nations; kings of people shall be of her. (Gen 17:15-16 KJV)**

So are some women suggesting that they themselves shouldn't be alive today, that none of us should be here today? Are they aware that they are criticizing what women accomplished? This is not about just aborting babies. It is ultimately about aborting future mothers and fathers, aborting future grandparents and grandchildren, aborting future workers, customers, entrepreneurs, managers, executives, lawyers, doctors, teachers, and so on. If a single person in your past had been aborted, everybody connected to that person, including you, would vanish. The removal of a single child has a significant effect on the economy 25 years in the future. This means that a single living person's suffering in the present can be directly tied to an abortion nearly 25 years in the past.

The problem here is people are not educated on how to handle a cause and an effect separated by 25 years. A female making a pro-abortion choice today is most likely making it for personal reasons. She is not given the moral foundation and the understanding of the impact her personal choice will have on the economic health of society, and herself, 25 years in the future. And the people who will be adversely affected by the abortion of this child are totally disconnected from this woman and her unborn child. So the million-dollar question is why would a company like Johnson & Johnson fund Planned Parenthood and also report massive layoffs due to collapsing sales and a vanishing customer base (not to mention a worker shortage)? Don't they also make baby products? This is a paradox worth investigating. At the very least, any support of abortion is a conflict of interest for us all.

> **And the LORD said unto Satan, Whence comest thou? Then Satan answered the LORD, and said, From going to and fro in the earth, and from walking up and down in it. (Job 1:7 KJV)**

The Truth About Women's Freedom

The truth however is that it's actually the opposite of what these women believe. The more children you have the more freedoms you have. The goal of the Satanic is to destroy God's people, those who represent Life. The first step is to get you to devalue Life. Even if you believe it's okay for others to have an abortion but maybe it isn't for you, then you have accepted the values of the Satanist. Life represents your God, and Life in abundance represents freedom. Regardless of what your religious beliefs are, the freedoms that you have must be protected. The protection of these freedoms is fought for and defended by the children you have and the children you will have. Your children are your future soldiers.

> **"And God blessed them, and God said unto them, Be fruitful, and multiply, and replenish the earth, and subdue it" (Genesis 1:28 KJV).**

> **As arrows are in the hand of a mighty man; so are children of the youth. [5] Happy is the man that hath his quiver full of them: they shall not be ashamed, but they shall speak with the enemies in the gate Psalm 127:4-5 KJV.**

America sealed its fate when it decided to legalize abortion. We have taken our freedoms for granted and now those who represent Death have control over our politics, media, schools, and economy. When you allow Death to pervade. It begins to destroy and spread like an uninhibited weed throughout all of your government systems.

With so many financial experts in America, a country that represents capitalism, there is never any mention of the economic impact of abortion. Again, the ones and zeros show up. Economic growth is tied to population growth. Economic decline is tied to population decline. America is on the verge of economic collapse because Life (1) has been removed.

As I stated above, by the end of my 12th grade year my future wife would become pregnant with my first son. She would have been a few months pregnant by the time I would depart for Marine Basic Military Training. Unknowingly, the birth of my first son would determine who I am and whom I'd become.

The Devil, or at the very least one of his minions, would advise my wife and me that we should abort my son. In his expert opinion, the child she was carrying would have a very difficult life, if he did survive. We were advised we'd spend our entire lives caring for him, as he would never be able to do anything for himself.

Nine months later she would deliver a healthy 6lb, 13oz baby boy. This would be the first of my first seven sons born and it wouldn't be the last time doctors would use fear to attempt to persuade us to do what they wanted and of course, I wouldn't listen to those doctors either. What I didn't know then but understand now, is that a person is truly the culmination of the decisions they make. I would go on to have six more children.

The choices you make in life define who you are. It's never about what a person says, it's about what he has done. Our choice not to abort was a stand against the Satanic program for the decline of humanity, particularly black humanity. Abortion must be opposed. The children of God must wake up and start obeying God's command to fill the earth.

When my wife and I made the decision to have our child, it wasn't made because of what I knew or understood about the world or the Bible. I only knew that I didn't want to do it. I was at an age when like most young adults, I didn't know what would happen next. This is an example of why obedience is important. I didn't have to understand why God wants us to be fruitful and multiply. We do not have to understand God's law, but in time we will. A child doesn't have to understand why they shouldn't touch a hot stove, what's important is their obedience to their parents. What's important for us as adults are our obedience to our Heavenly Father.

The New Testament law is Love and the Old Testament is the standard for Love. This is to say that loyalty and obedience always look like love, but love doesn't always look like loyalty and obedience.

Gay Marriage

The next social phenomenon that is leading to a collapse is gay marriage. More specifically, it is the undermining of traditional marriage. The problem came about when marriage ceased to be the definition of something and began to be a word to be defined. As a definition, *marriage* is what you call what happens when a godly man who is going along in life with God, fulfilling his purpose to produce on the earth, subduing it according to the way God designed and called him to do, and a woman comes along who loves him and wants to help him fulfill the purpose God had given him, adding also the other dimension of the Cultural Mandate (Gen 1:28), to produce offspring. She is brought to him as a helper "meet for him," his helpmeet.

> **18 And the Lord God said, It is not good that the man should be alone; I will make him an help meet for him.**
>
> **19 And out of the ground the Lord God formed every beast of the field, and every fowl of the air; and brought them unto Adam to see what he would call them: and whatsoever Adam called every living creature, that was the name thereof.**
>
> **20 And Adam gave names to all cattle, and to the fowl of the air, and to every beast of the field; but for Adam there was not found an help meet for him.**
>
> **21 And the Lord God caused a deep sleep to fall upon Adam, and he slept: and he took one of his ribs, and closed up the flesh instead thereof;**
>
> **22 And the rib, which the Lord God had taken from man, made he a woman, and brought her unto the man.**

> **[23] And Adam said, This is now bone of my bones, and flesh of my flesh: she shall be called Woman, because she was taken out of Man.**
>
> **[24] Therefore shall a man leave his father and his mother, and shall cleave unto his wife: and they shall be one flesh. (Gen 2:18-24 KJV)**

What do you call this? The word is *marriage.* Marriage is the definition of this thing: a man and woman, joined together by God for life and for raising a godly family.

But marriage ceased to be a definition when elements of mankind began to see it as a word that itself needed to be defined. The first view we have discussed is called the *conjugal view* of marriage. That phrase is wrapped up in the procreation aspect of the term. But the "new" view is the *revisionist* view. This view centers on the false idea that the *reason* for marriage is to make one happy. These terms were first coined by Sherif Girgis, Ryan T. Anderson, and Robert P. George in their helpful book, *What is Marriage? Man and Woman: A Defense.*

CITATION: Sherif Girgis, Ryan T. Anderson, and Robert P. George, What Is Marriage? Man and Woman: A Defense (New York: Encounter Books)

How did this come about? It came along with the "reforms" of women's lib. While it should be noted that this is a complex issue, we have to wrestle with the implications. The first culprit in the redefinition of marriage is "no-fault divorce." Most would hale this innovation (and it is indeed a recent innovation) as a win for happiness and for oppressed women. But is it? In America before 1969 when Ronald Reagan signed the first bills into law (a decision he later called a mistake), in order to obtain a divorce, one had to prove there were adequate grounds for the divorce, a "fault" with the other person. The reason is that the courts understood that our whole society and the stability thereof depended on families that were intact. If only for the sake of our children, the courts were very reluctant to break up a family.

But today in America, no-fault divorce is the rule. While this actually had some positive effects (lowering cases of domestic violence and suicide among married women) for obvious reasons, the negative effects are still playing out.

> First of all, couples who might very well work out their differences under a stronger commitment have too much incentive to call it quits.
>
> Second, as stated before, children are the biggest losers in such cases.

Tellingly, the first country to enact no-fault divorce laws of the current magnitude was Russia after the revolution. Why? They saw marriage as a bourgeois institution and thought that marriage and the nuclear family undermined the state. It should be noted that the very first of such laws was enacted in Prussia in 1757 in the case of severe disharmony between the two parties of a childless couple. The fact the communists were the first to enact the laws for married couples with children says a lot about what Satan stands to benefit from such laws.

But this is a section on gay marriage. So how does no-fault divorce lead to gay marriage? The answer is simple. When marriage ceased to be the defining word that described a union between a man and his wife in order to raise a family, and instead became a romantic union between two people for the sake of becoming happy, the door opened wide to who could enter into this "union of a happy romance." If marriage is nothing but a romantic union for the sake of happiness, then "love who you love."

This is why it is so difficult to fight this redefinition politically or legally. Why shouldn't the state allow gay marriage if it is just romance and companionship for the sake of happiness? On what grounds could they prevent it? If a majority of voters were conservative children of God and voted together against it, would that not be a union of church and state? Are we not legislating morality in an arbitrary way according to majority rule? You might ask what is wrong with that. But it would not be a good way forward, because whenever we are legislating morality that we are unable to tie back to fundamental axiomatic laws (such as do not murder, and do not steal), then we are at the mercy of the whims of the majority. What happens when the majority are of the beast? Do we want a pure democracy then?

But the power of the American Constitution is that it makes us a nation under a rule of law—that is—we are a nation ruled by laws, not by men. Men are elected to enforce the laws to which we are beholden.

But not to forget we are discussing marriage. The goal would be to define marriage properly so that it falls under these fundamental axioms. To do that, you look at the creation of male and female, and then the union of male and female. In Genesis 1:26-28 it says:

[26] And God said, Let us make man in our image, after our likeness: and let them have dominion over the fish of the sea, and over the fowl of the air, and over the cattle, and over all the earth, and over every creeping thing that creepeth upon the earth.

[27] So God created man in his own image, in the image of God created he him; *male and female* created he them.

[28] And God blessed them, and God said unto them, *Be fruitful, and multiply, and replenish the earth, and subdue it:* and have dominion over the fish of the sea, and over the fowl of the air, and over every living thing that moveth upon the earth. (KJV emphasis added)

Remember that the whole Bible is about God asking man one question: Do you want life, or do you want death? The first time he asks it is just before he creates the institution of marriage in Genesis 2:15-17.

[15] And the Lord God took the man, and put him into the garden of Eden to dress it and to keep it.

[16] And the Lord God commanded the man, saying, Of every tree of the garden thou mayest freely eat:

[17] But of the tree of the knowledge of good and evil, thou shalt not eat of it: for in the day that thou eatest thereof thou shalt surely die.

Freely eat any tree here but one, and you will live. Eat of this tree and you will die. Live or die. That is always the choice. And embedded in the choice to live is the choice to obey God's commands to produce offspring. The very next verses say:

> **18 And the Lord God said, It is not good that the man should be alone; I will make him an help meet for him.**
>
> **19 And out of the ground the Lord God formed every beast of the field, and every fowl of the air; and brought them unto Adam to see what he would call them: and whatsoever Adam called every living creature, that was the name thereof.**
>
> **20 And Adam gave names to all cattle, and to the fowl of the air, and to every beast of the field; but for Adam there was not found an help meet for him.**
>
> **21 And the Lord God caused a deep sleep to fall upon Adam, and he slept: and he took one of his ribs, and closed up the flesh instead thereof;**
>
> **22 And the rib, which the Lord God had taken from man, made he a woman, and brought her unto the man.**
>
> **23 And Adam said, This is now bone of my bones, and flesh of my flesh: she shall be called Woman, because she was taken out of Man.**
>
> **24 Therefore shall a man leave his father and his mother, and shall cleave unto his wife: and they shall be one flesh.**
>
> **25 And they were both naked, the man and his wife, and were not ashamed. (Gen 2:18-25)**

Adam has learned an important lesson about life. It involves finding a wife "meet for him," which means, "fit for him." This is a good place to point out that this "fit" starts with sexuality. A man is not a fit for a man. When two men fit together it is rightly called "unnatural." To make it "fit" requires a dangerous and gross deviation. This is also true for two women. They don't "fit" at all. Women who love women romantically are often fed up with men. What they want is someone they can relate to. In their brokenness, they look for the sympathy of one who is just like them. But being the same is not being a fit. Men and women complement one another, starting with their sexual organs. I don't need to say anything else.

Marriage then is the special relationship between two who are "meet" for one another, largely for the sake of doing what God created man to do: multiply, fill, and subdue the creation in the name of God, in whom and for whom we have been given a delegated authority. But in separating from God, we have rebelled against that ultimate authority and gone rogue, losing our position as his delegates. Imagine a policeman who goes rogue, takes off his badge, and starts arresting people on his own authority. He has no right. The only way we can take up our position with God again is to return to him and to his rule—his law. In return, we return marriage to its rightful place as a definition, not a word to be defined.

The children of Satan can do what they want. If two men want to love each other and have sex with each other, there is no reason to stop them. Evil will do what evil will do. But the children of God can not be lulled into a belief that it is a kindness to endorse the abomination. Many liberal "Christians" will say that the Bible does not prohibit or judge homosexuality. This is simply a lie. Both the Old and New Testaments make it extremely clear that two people of the same sex are *not* "meet" for one another (though they may be "meat" for one another). That Christians are even debating this shows the degree to which the evil one has infiltrated the church.

But what must be considered now is the current custom for the state to be the entity that sanctions the marital union. Perhaps this is where we have mostly gone wrong. This is why there is a debate now. The state gets to define marriage because the state gets to judge the legitimacy of the union. In some ways, this is proper. The state is supposed to be an agent of God. In

Romans 13 it says,

> **1 Let every soul be subject unto the higher powers. For there is no power but of God: the powers that be are ordained of God.**
>
> **2 Whosoever therefore resisteth the power, resisteth the ordinance of God: and they that resist shall receive to themselves damnation.**
>
> **3 For rulers are not a terror to good works, but to the evil. Wilt thou then not be afraid of the power? do that which is good, and thou shalt have praise of the same:**
>
> **4 For he is the minister of God to thee for good. But if thou do that which is evil, be afraid; for he beareth not the sword in vain: for he is the minister of God, a revenger to execute wrath upon him that doeth evil.**
>
> **5 Wherefore ye must needs be subject, not only for wrath, but also for conscience sake.**

> 6 **For for this cause pay ye tribute also: for they are God's ministers, attending continually upon this very thing.**
>
> 7 **Render therefore to all their dues: tribute to whom tribute is due; custom to whom custom; fear to whom fear; honour to whom honour. (Ro 13:1-7)**

If we are to take Paul seriously here, he is saying no matter how corrupt, the government is put in place by God, who is sovereign over all things. In some ways, this is hard to grasp. But it does speak to the proper role of a government that is not a theocracy. The Jews were governed by theocracy. In the time of the judges, God was their king. Their civil laws were God's laws. The United States is not meant to be a theocracy. Separating church and state was proper in the origination of our country because the Founders had already seen the carnage of a secular state with a state religion. The First Amendment of the Constitution

> "provides that Congress make no law respecting an establishment of religion or prohibiting its free exercise. It protects freedom of speech, the press, assembly, and the right to petition the Government for a redress of grievances."

In his letter on January 1, 1802, Thomas Jefferson addressed the Danbury Baptist Association in Connecticut,

> Believing with you that religion is a matter which lies solely between Man & his God, that he owes account to none other for his faith or his worship, that the legitimate powers of government reach actions only, & not opinions,

> I contemplate with sovereign reverence that act of the whole American people which declared that their legislature should "make no law respecting an establishment of religion, or prohibiting the free exercise thereof," thus building a wall of separation between Church & State. Adhering to this expression of the supreme will of the nation on behalf of the rights of conscience, I shall see with sincere satisfaction the progress of those sentiments which tend to restore to man all his natural rights, convinced he has no natural right in opposition to his social duties."

They understood that any compulsion of religion would nullify the faith of the individual. God wants his children to choose him freely or not at all. Going back to Paul's letter to the Romans, though, in spite of the separation of Church and State, the government is a benefit to its citizens who do not have to take the law into their own hands, because when there is a representative government, the state is an agent of God for establishing laws, enforcing laws, and enforcing contracts between its citizens. The state should be beholden to axiomatic laws. Men should not make arbitrary laws by majority vote, which is what we currently see more and more. The state, in a proper government, has a monopoly on the initiation of force, and it is only to use that force to protect its citizens from the use of force by others, police for citizens against citizens, and the military for the country against country. There will be more discussion on this in chapter 9.

Back to Marriage

In light of all that, there is a case that when the state recognizes the legality and legitimacy of a marriage, it is functioning as God's agent. Marriage is a fundamental axiom given in the first pages of the Bible. But when the state begins to make arbitrary decisions that redefine marriage, then it steps outside its role. The state can redefine marriage all it wants, but God will never recognize such a redefinition, and neither can the children of God. Now that the state is corrupt, the citizens have no choice but to accept the laws. When Paul wrote the Romans to submit to the government, they were dealing with a much more corrupt government than we are at this time and place in history.

So what should children of God do when the state makes unbiblical laws? In the case of gay marriage, the children of God should look to the Bible, not the state for moral clarity. So the state legalizes gay marriage. The child of God is not to engage in gay marriage or homosexuality. It is not for the children of God to subvert the government in this case. Meaning, that it is not for the children of God to take up arms and attempt to overthrow the government. Just as in the case of abortion, we simply would not have an abortion for any reason, though the government allows it.

"Marriage is honourable in all, and the bed undefiled" (Heb 13:4a KJV). We must hold the marriage bed sacred and undefiled, but the children of Satan are nowhere near done defiling the marriage bed, and we will likely see things get worse. The philosophical door that has been unlocked and opened by the redefinition of marriage to the revisionist view will allow for all kinds of evil. What kind of romance makes the Beast happy? Is it multiple partners? Is it children? Is it animals and inanimate objects, or perhaps trees? Use your imagination. The only thing that matters is happiness.

Herding and Depopulation

What has been going on in recent years could be referred to as *herding*, which makes it difficult for those who live in urban areas to see. Herding is hard to notice if you live in an urban environment because it is in the urban environment that people are being herded.

Simply put, the small and medium-sized towns are dying as viable jobs in those communities become more and more scarce. One major reason for this is the advent of industrial farming. Thousands of communities were brought into existence as the western frontier was being won in America, and the lifeblood of those communities were the farms and the families who worked them. While it is true that industrial farming has created more food using fewer people, it is also true that this created a problem for those who once farmed those same lands, mainly, that way of life was rendered obsolete. This was a way of life where fathers passed down land and the wisdom to cultivate it for generations. Sons didn't go out to find an identity, they were born into it.

Farms didn't just grow one cash crop, like today, but were diverse and well-managed ecosystems, perpetuating fertility and fruitfulness year after year by crop rotation and wise management. Sons could count on their fathers leaving it to them better than their fathers had left it, with the mantle passed for the sons to do the same.

It took more than one family per county to make a farm productive, so the community was built up around several families who helped each other, worshiped in church together, and educated their children together. Towns need grocers, barbers, doctors, druggists, and all manner of tradesmen, and there was room to grow and to prosper together in these communities, which made up the counties, which made up the states, and made up a great country.

But with progress came the death of these towns. One corporation owns the land that was once owned by ten or twenty families. When those families lost their sons to the cities, the few who stayed behind saw their schools, churches, and stores shuttered. In many of these communities, the only thriving ministry is the meth labs and liquor stores. In another generation, many of these towns will be in total ruins.

Another interesting and terrifying point is that the corporations who are buying American farmland are Chinese and Russian. Why is this important?

The problem with communist corporations buying American land and businesses is that it hides the fact that it's China and Russia who actually owns your food production because, under communism, the state owns everything. The individual owns nothing, and what he thinks he owns can be taken by the state on a whim.

So what we have is Americans competing with a foreign country. America is already overthrown. Our leaders are compromised, and it doesn't matter who you vote for, but that's another matter.

Currently, China owns America's largest pork producer located in Smithfield, VA, Smithfield Foods. This accomplishes multiple goals for China. One is a controlled demolition of America. If left alone everyone would notice disappearing people.

As the population is reduced, production has to be reduced. According to Bank of America, there are currently 2 jobs available for every American, and in 2008, it said there were 6.5 people for each job available.

We have crossed over and fallen off of the population cliff. When the lights go out, they're going to make it as difficult as possible for God's people to survive. The water is polluted, the food is contaminated, and bad seeds and fertilizers will make survival difficult. We're at war and we're losing. It's sad that nobody notices it and women are fighting to kill more of their children, which is aiding the enemy in their war.

Walmart

Somewhere in the midst of all this collapse of family farms and the towns that supported them, Walmart opened stores all over the country, including rural areas, and boosted jobs for many, while destroying the mom and pop stores and the self-employed. After destroying the local economy, along with a shrinking population, Walmart's closures meant the end for some of these areas in places where it was the largest employer.

And where does everyone go? To the cities, but the cities don't seem to be prospering either. Now we have a shortage of workers, skilled and unskilled. There is a low unemployment rate being reported, but at the same time, it is reported that people don't want to come to work, and there are a record number of job openings. These two points are never reconciled.

Even four years ago, Detroit was celebrating the demolition of 10,000 homes and was excited to raze even more. The pandemic was an attempt to hide this alarming decrease in population. That was at least one of the nefarious purposes on the government's agenda. Social distancing and store closures can now be blamed on the pandemic instead of the truth. Which is that men and women made a conscious decision to not have children and engage in lifestyles that don't produce children. This along with the fact that since the legalization of Roe vs. Wade over 60 million children have been aborted. The reality that children in large numbers were never born will appear to many as the Rapture when they finally have eyes to see that the world they live in has many people who aren't here. Somehow everyone knows where babies come from, but no one knows where people come from.

We are now at a point of no return. Each year our high schools will have a smaller and smaller graduating class as the current culture doesn't want kids. We've aborted our future of freedom and now we're in a spiral where each year there are fewer people available to have children.

Automation, self-checkout, and bots that answer corporate calls are your missing children.

Unless the children of God start doing what they are called to do and begin "multiplying" at a high rate, we will more and more make up the minority and see the nation's laws get further and further away from God's law. Hold the marriage bed sacred (Heb 13:4). Get back to the biblical, conjugal definition of marriage. Better yet, don't define marriage. Let it be as God created it, the word that defines something—the unbreakable union between a man and his wife for the sake of serving God together, multiplying together, and covering the face of the earth with the righteous children of God.

Chapter 7

Religion is Not Helping

"How can you have order in a state without religion? For, when one man is dying of hunger near another who is ill of surfeit, he cannot resign himself to this difference unless there is an authority which declares 'God wills it thus.' Religion is excellent stuff for keeping common people quiet."

~ Napoleon Bonaparte

Religion is whatever you believe and those beliefs manifest as culture. Culture is the extension of the mind. Culture is what a group of people has established as normal. You change a culture by changing what people believe and that truth will manifest itself in the world around you. We have accepted the idea that you are either religious or secular. This idea is misleading because this isn't the truth of the world. Some associate secularism with being neutral. There isn't any option for neutrality, you are either for God or against God. Abstaining from doing anything is disobedience to God because He told you to do something. Silence in the presence of evil is disobedience. The truth is that everyone has a religion. Everyone has a set of beliefs, and that's your religion. Just because your individual beliefs aren't prepackaged as one of today's mainstream doctrines doesn't mean that you don't have a religion.

Robert Capon, who was a pastor and author, wrote this about religion,

> Religion is the attempt on the part of human beings to establish a right relationship between themselves and something outside themselves–something they think to be of life-shaping importance. Notice that I have deliberately left most of the details out of this definition. The nature of the attempt is yet to be specified: it could involve thoughts, words, or deeds, and it could entail anything from meditating on a mantra to feeding your firstborn to crocodiles. Likewise, the right relationship is still undefined: it might be one of harmony and union, or of cautiousness and control, or even of fear and total avoidance. Finally, something outside themselves is very much up for grabs: it could be God, or the goddess, or the gods, or Satan; but it could also be nature, happiness, fate, the forces of the universe, the spirits of the dead–or, to my point in this book, health, money, or love.
>
> In any case, in this definition, religion is an attempt to influence someone or something; and it invariably results in the creation of a program designed to exert such influence. This program may be about God, the good life, or good sex. It may be strenuous or relaxed. It may call for the commitment of a lifetime or need only the whim of a moment. But whatever it's incidental variations of goal or style, it will always have three essential characteristics: it

will involve a creed; it will demand specific cultic practices, and it will insist on certain patterns of conduct in its adherents. Creed, Cult, and Conduct, then–the three Cs of the program of religion. Let me flesh them out briefly.

Creed encompasses everything we think (or believe, to use the word loosely) when we undertake the program of a particular religion. Such thoughts may involve subjects as diverse as God, money, Satan, or jogging for your health. They may amount to nothing more than vague attitudes of approval or disapproval, or they may entail subscription to the entire body of formal doctrine. "The universe is nice," for example, it's a possible creed…In every case, though, each such creed will turn out to be a formula for thinking about the "something outside ourselves"…

Cult stands for all the liturgical practices our religion's program calls for. These can range from chicken sacrifices at dawn, to Morning Prayer and Sermon on Sundays, to not eating saturated fats, to transcendental meditation, to owning a house in the Hamptons. At first glance, this spectrum of practices may look like nothing more than individual preference at work; but in fact, the particular "liturgies" we engage in are almost always dictated socially, by our coreligionists–by our fellow Episcopalians, possibly, or by our fellow health nuts, or by our fellow yuppies…In the last analysis, therefore, all such practices, conventionally pious or not, are undertaken precisely for religious reasons: we do them on the assumption (once again) that if we get them right, the relationship we are seeking to establish will become a reality.

> Conduct, finally, covers the rest of the territory of religion: it stands generally for the behavioral requirements that the program of our religion lays upon us, but specifically for the moral aspects of those requirements...Depending on the particulars of our program, we could earn a religious good conduct medal by having one wife, or two wives, or none–or simply by never marrying our mother-in-law. We could give all our goods to the poor or we could keep them for ourselves...Or–to run out the list at random–we could lift weights, eat yogurt, wear garlic around our necks, or not step on sidewalk cracks. But once again, and for the last time: every one of these things–when done as part of the program of religion–would be done on the assumption that if we got it right, it would land us in the New Jerusalem, or the Old Eden, or the Good Life–or whatever state our religion names as the fulfillment of the relationship we desire.
>
> (Health, Money, and Love and Why We Don't Enjoy Them)

Capon's aim is to end our obsession with religion by proving that Christ came to end religion and bring us into a right relationship with God. But I would say he is correct in his explanation of the inherent religiousness of humanity, whether the children of God or of Satan. That said, where preachers like Capon might advocate for the crucifixion of the law, I would advocate for the keeping of the law. However, that is not to say that he has no point.

When I advocate for the keeping of the laws of God, as I have for this entire book, I am not talking about some cult, creed, and conduct for the sake of earning the right relationship with God. This would be to see religion and obedience as a *duty*. I am not advocating for duty-bound religion. What I am advocating for is an understanding of *causality*. God's ways are not arbitrary. All of his commands pertain to the securing of Life and the avoidance of Death. Do we eat every day out of duty? Or do we eat out of causality? Isn't it true that if we do not eat, we will die soon? This is the cause and effect. Doesn't God show that he is about cause and effect when he throws out all of his "if-then" statements about life and death, beginning with, "*If* you eat of it, *then* you will surely die?"

Religion is not helping, because almost all forms of Christianity and Judaism, not to mention Islam, Buddhism, Hinduism, and Bahai, (list your favorite religion here) all frame their tenants around *duty*.

Duty says you *should* live a certain way so that God won't be mad at you. That is not the point. Surely, God does get angry when we ignore his ways, but even more, it makes him sad. Why? Because he is a good Father. What good parent among us doesn't lament to see our children fail to listen to our wisdom and thereby destroy themselves by causality? We teach them how not to die, and they see it as rules, rather than the words of Life. If that doesn't make you sad, you don't have a heart. God has a heart. When Jesus contemplated Jerusalem's failure to obey God, he said,

> **O Jerusalem, Jerusalem, thou that killest the prophets, and stonest them which are sent unto thee, how often would I have gathered thy children together, even as a hen gathereth her chickens under her wings, and ye would not! (Matthew 23:37 KJV)**

God prompted the prophet Jeremiah to write an entire prophetic book of Lamentation. All the prophets lament because God laments. It is a tragedy that God has made a way for his children to receive Life abundantly, and we have chosen Death instead because a religion of duty was too difficult. When we make it about duty, we see God's ways as arbitrary, as a difficult, actually impossible task. We cling to the gospel of grace because we think following God is impossible.

I am all for clinging to the grace of God. We need his forgiveness and unfailing love. We need God to give us second chances. We are slow to learn and rely on the patience of God. And the Bible shows that God is patient, but he is not infinitely patient, because judgment and consequence do come eventually. Slow to anger he is, but he does anger.

> **19 And when the Lord saw it, he abhorred them, because of the provoking of his sons, and of his daughters.**
>
> **20 And he said, I will hide my face from them, I will see what their end shall be: for they are a very froward generation, children in whom is no faith.**
>
> **21 They have moved me to jealousy with that which is not God; they have provoked me to anger with their vanities: and I will move them to jealousy with those which are not a people; I will provoke them to anger with a foolish nation.**
>
> **22 For a fire is kindled in mine anger, and shall burn unto the lowest hell, and shall consume the earth with her increase, and set on fire the foundations of the mountains.**

23 I will heap mischiefs upon them; I will spend mine arrows upon them.

24 They shall be burnt with hunger, and devoured with burning heat, and with bitter destruction: I will also send the teeth of beasts upon them, with the poison of serpents of the dust.

25 The sword without, and terror within, shall destroy both the young man and the virgin, the suckling also with the man of gray hairs.

26 I said, I would scatter them into corners, I would make the remembrance of them to cease from among men:

27 Were it not that I feared the wrath of the enemy, lest their adversaries should behave themselves strangely, and lest they should say, Our hand is high, and the Lord hath not done all this.

28 For they are a nation void of counsel, neither is there any understanding in them.

29 O that they were wise, that they understood this, that they would consider their latter end!

30 How should one chase a thousand, and two put ten thousand to flight, except their Rock had sold them, and the Lord had shut them up?

31 For their rock is not as our Rock, even our enemies themselves being judges.

[32] For their vine is of the vine of Sodom, and of the fields of Gomorrah: their grapes are grapes of gall, their clusters are bitter:

[33] Their wine is the poison of dragons, and the cruel venom of asps.

[34] Is not this laid up in store with me, and sealed up among my treasures? (Deuteronomy 32:19-34)

[5] Thou shalt not bow down thyself to them, nor serve them: for I the Lord thy God am a jealous God, visiting the iniquity of the fathers upon the children unto the third and fourth generation of them that hate me; (Exodus 20:5)

Exodus 34:6-7 shows the full nature and character of God.

[6] And the Lord passed by before him, and proclaimed, The Lord, The Lord God, merciful and gracious, longsuffering, and abundant in goodness and truth,

[7] Keeping mercy for thousands, forgiving iniquity and transgression and sin, and that will by no means clear the guilty; visiting the iniquity of the fathers upon the children, and upon the children's children, unto the third and to the fourth generation.

The Lord is indeed merciful, gracious, long-suffering, and abundant in goodness and truth. He does keep mercy for thousands and forgives. But it also warns that he will by no means clear the guilty. Interestingly, this shows the likelihood that if we don't follow God, neither will our children and when they don't, their lives will show the results of that. There is nothing more important than modeling righteousness and teaching our children by our example to follow God and keep to his ways. We've given them Death if we don't.

Religion is Not the Point

Religion isn't helping, because religion always makes religion the point. Consider the state of the Church right now. The message has little to do with following God in obedience, and when it does, the picture of what obedience looks like is totally unclear. Each church has its pet doctrines and rules which if followed supposedly put someone into that right relationship with God. And what are those rules? Show up to the church, pray, read your Bible, maybe don't look at pornography, and don't cuss. Oh, and be sure to give a lot of money to the church.

But what they love to talk about more than anything is the impossible and infinite standard of perfection that God expects. They'll say, you have to be perfect, and only God can be perfect, so give up trying, just pray a prayer to get Jesus into your heart, and be very committed to church with your time and money. Every sermon is some version of "God's standard is impossibly high, run to the cross for forgiveness. Run to the church for a consolation when you can't actually follow God." It is lucrative for the church. It is not lucrative to see you change, only to see you dependent on the church.

What About Those Who Don't Go to Church?

Those who consider themselves non-religious have simply accepted the world views that they were taught. What's interesting is that we've all been indoctrinated with the same world views to the point where it has either moved us away from the Bible or made the Bible difficult to understand. It's because of this, that many now consider themselves non-religious, or why many who are religious have adopted behaviors and beliefs that are secular, such as being pro-choice and Christian.

God is "Truth," and when you're given truth you are moved closer to God. "Knowledge" moves you away from God. This is what makes knowledge dangerous. If you do not know where the information is coming from, or the intent of those giving it to you, then you become vulnerable. The Covid-19 vaccinations were a display of secular faith in the government.

No one knows the long-term effects of the vaccine, and the ingredients which are required by law to be on the bottle weren't present. Yet many people lined up to take the shot. The only thing they needed to hear from the CDC were the same words spoken to Eve, "ye shall not surely die" (Gen 3:4).

What is present in all things is a duality. There are those who have faith in God and those who have secular faith. Secular faith is having trust in the knowledge of anything other than God.

> *"We Jews have erred grievously. We who have posed as having given the world 'the' Saviour, are today nothing else than its destroyers, its incendiaries, its executioners. We, who have promised you a New Heaven, have given you a New Hell".*
>
> **–Dr. Oscar Levy, in "The World Significance of the Russian Revolution".**

The more things change, the more they stay the same. The same people who gave you the knowledge of good and evil, are the same people who gave you the vaccination. They're the same people who crucified Jesus, gave you the New Testament, and established the Roman Catholic Church. The world is still dealing with the Romans and Jews today.

Revelation 2:9

> **I know thy works, and tribulation, and poverty, (but thou art rich) and I know the blasphemy of them which say they are Jews, and are not, but are the synagogue of Satan.**

Revelation 3:9

> **Behold, I will make them of the synagogue of Satan, which say they are Jews, and are not, but do lie;**

Today's communists are yesterday's Romans. These are the same people who are today manipulating world events, holding high seats in world governments, educating our children, and feeding us with news. It is the Romans in today's political offices who are pushing vaccination and controlling America's politics. It's the Romans who create problems so that they may offer you the solution, a socialist solution.

In 1919, President Woodrow Wilson and Attorney General Alexander Palmer sought to remove America's Romans and deport them. America has a history with this group and during WWII, thousands were considered enemy aliens.

The Romans today continue to persecute the followers of Jesus, including Christian Jews. They gave you the New Testament so that they could kill you. This explains why the Christians have the cross and the image of the Satanist is the double cross. The goal is to move you away from the law and towards the love of your enemy. This doesn't mean that Jesus is the problem. The problem is that Jesus didn't write the story. He didn't have to. In Jesus' exchange with Satan multiple times he says, "it is written." (Matthew 4:4,7,10).

Because the words that man needs are already written, there's no need for Jesus to write the law again as he states, "Think not that I am come to destroy the law, or the prophets: I am not come to destroy, but to fulfill" (Mt 5:17).

Since Jesus' intent is not to undo the law, this means we are to continue to follow OT laws. If you choose to continue to follow NT teachings of love and forgiveness, you can't forget that it's Law before Love. The love and forgiveness that you have, should be reserved for God's people, not the beast. There may be a sense that we "love" our enemies, in the way you might love and not hate an enemy combatant, or one who has earned a seat on the electric chair. It is right to judge without hate in your heart, but one still much judge justly.

The Romans who gave you the NT knowledge did something that, "Truth", doesn't do, and that's divide, division being a mark of the beast. Once God's people were given a NT, a new choice, you immediately have division. The NT divided its followers, some remained Mosaic Jews while others became "Christian."

Since we have established that the world has a duality, we know that if there is a mark of the beast, then there must be a Mark of God. The marks of the beast are many and they are anything that isn't the Mark of God. God's Marks are cleanliness, law, life, liberty, unity, health, order, and truth. The marks of the beast are filth, slavery, division, lawlessness, death, disease, disorder, and deception.

This helps us explain the following verses in the OT and NT.

Genesis 9:4 Old Testament

But flesh with the life thereof, which is the blood thereof, shall ye not eat.

John 6:31-34 New Testament

[31] Our fathers did eat manna in the desert; as it is written, He gave them bread from heaven to eat. 32 Then Jesus said unto them, Verily, verily, I say unto you, Moses gave you not that bread from heaven; but my Father giveth you the true bread from heaven. 33 For the bread of God is he which cometh down from heaven, and giveth life unto the world. 34 Then said they unto him, Lord, evermore give us this bread.

John 6:41 New Testament

The Jews then murmured at him, because he said, I am the bread which came down from heaven.

John 6:53-56 New Testament

[53] Then Jesus said unto them, Verily, verily, I say unto you, Except ye eat the flesh of the Son of man, and drink his blood, ye have no life in you. [54] Whoso eateth my flesh, and drinketh my blood, hath eternal life; and I will raise him up at the last day. [55] For my flesh is meat indeed, and my blood is drink indeed. [56] He that eateth my flesh, and drinketh my blood, dwelleth in me, and I in him.

What we have is the OT warning you about a NT. There is One Creator and One Law. God is that authority, His authority is Law. God created Heaven and Earth before he created man, which means the laws that are in the design existed before we were created and will exist after our death. This is why the Bible can warn God's children about what comes next.

Deuteronomy 30:10-13 Old Testament

> **10 If thou shalt hearken unto the voice of the LORD thy God,
> to keep his commandments and his statutes which are written
> in this book of the law, and if thou turn unto the LORD thy
> God with all thine heart, and with all thy soul. 11 For this
> commandment which I command thee this day, it is not
> hidden from thee, neither is it far off. 12 It is not in heaven, that
> thou shouldest say, Who shall go up for us to heaven, and bring
> it unto us, that we may hear it, and do it? 13 Neither is it beyond
> the sea, that thou shouldest say, Who shall go over the sea for
> us, and bring it unto us, that we may hear it, and do it?**

The words that Jesus spoke were not meant to be taken literally to mean, "eat of the Son of Man's flesh and drink of his blood." He was communicating that following Jesus and his teachings is the spirit that gives you eternal life, life after death. What is to be noted is that there are men and women among us who do these things. They eat the flesh and drink the blood of men, women, and children. These are the beasts who seek to turn children of God away from the law.

The OT covenant doesn't reward you with life after death. The reward of law is life, life in abundance, and liberty, before death. It is the enemy of God's people who want them to wait for death to seek God's reward of Heaven. In doing so, you break God's covenant, which is maintaining God's laws on Earth. You're also not doing the very thing He told you to do in Genesis 1:28, which is to subdue the Earth.

The OT warns you, that you become what you worship, and that you are to worship the Creator and not the created. You are not to worship graven images, money, or anything man has created. What we see today are men and women who worship money and other created things and images, and now they have no eyes to see, or ears to hear. They now belong to the congregation of the dead. The Creator is 'Life'.

Proverbs 21:16 KJV

The man that wandereth out of the way of understanding shall remain in the congregation of the dead.

Psalm 115:3-8

But our God is in the heavens: he hath done whatsoever he hath pleased. [4] Their idols are silver and gold, the work of men's hands. [5] They have mouths, but they speak not: eyes have they, but they see not: [6] They have ears, but they hear not: noses have they, but they smell not: [7] They have hands, but they handle not: feet have they, but they walk not: neither speak they through their throat. [8] They that make them are like unto them; so is every one that trusteth in them.

Romans 1:25-26

Who changed the truth of God into a lie, and worshipped and served the creature more than the Creator, who is blessed for ever. Amen. [26] For this cause God gave them up unto vile

affections: for even their women did change the natural use into that which is against nature:

I'm not trying to turn people away from Christ. People with beliefs are generally on the good side. Satan's worshipers are making us fight each other. But many Christians have been deceived and are fighting on the wrong side. This is what I hope to address with this book.

A Word About the Afterlife

As I said before, the trick of the Romans is to direct attention away from this Life and onto the afterlife. This was no doubt easy to do when the average life expectancy was 35, infant mortality was high, and pain and suffering were the inevitable result of much time on earth.

Whatever happens in the afterlife is a mystery? Even those who claim it is clearly described in Scripture would be hard-pressed to prove that point on a careful reading. I have no intention of convincing the reader that there is no afterlife.

However…

One mistake that we must not make in our desire for life after death, is to give up living in this world. Gurus and philosophers for centuries have done us a disservice by teaching us that real life is in some spiritual realm and that this dirty, filthy, material life is not real. This has been one of Satan's most powerful tricks. When Eve and then Adam bit into the fruit of "knowledge," this is the kind of garbage they learned in their university Ph.D. programs.

One of the first and most notable to make this assertion was Plato, who taught that "forms" were the real stuff of which life and material on earth were only a shadow. People eat this crap up, and it teaches them to walk in contradictions and to mistrust logic and objectivity. But logic and objectivity are the very things we need if we are going to trade "knowledge" for *knowing*, that is if we are going to trade sophistry for Truth.

Once we have been taught that we cannot trust our eyes and ears on earth then we have no basis for godly and sound judgment. Now we'll believe anything our handlers tell us. It is notable that it was also Plato who believed that the "masses" of ordinary people were too stupid to rule themselves or have a relationship with God. They needed wise philosopher kings like Barack Obama to rule them by his enlightened ability to understand all the contradictions of philosophy— to tell them, "You will not surely die…" and to show them how to live.

This is religion at its finest. Trade religion for truth if you're able.

Chapter 8

The Art of War, Communism, and Globalism

Here's an intriguing part of history. There are three types of Jews. Mosaic Jews, Christian Jews, and Satanic Jews.

After realizing that today's world is about the duality of good vs evil. I then had to review history using this biblical standard. What then becomes clear is that unlike what has been taught in schools there was never a Jewish Holocaust, it was a Christian Holocaust. I don't mean that I am minimizing the horrors of Nazi concentration camps and that millions of Jews were killed. But this is the only way to make sense of the players who participated in these World Wars.

This conflict is unusual in that, while Germany and Russia were engaged in a war they were killing their citizens. Germany did kill Jews but Germany was Christian. And Russian leaders killed Russians who were also Christian.

The victors write history, so instead of it being called the Christian Holocaust, it's the Jewish Holocaust. So far I haven't said much about the Jews. I have reverence for God-fearing Jews like Moses and anyone today who lives by the truth. But there have always been Satanic Jews since the Israelites fled Egypt.

Russia and Ukraine

Satanic Jews have blood on their hands and have been killing followers of Jesus since the day they put him on the cross. War in the past has been used by countries to get rid of certain people. This is what's happening in the war between Russia and Ukraine today. The Jews of these two countries are allies, they're not enemies. Putin is not an enemy of America and Ukraine's Jewish leader Zalensky is not an enemy of communism or its allies, and they're all on the same page.

Today's war is the state vs the people. The Ukraine war has brought financial pressure to everyone in the world. That's what they (the Satanic Jews) intended to do.

What I want you to understand is that no matter how comfortable you are right now, the enemy is coming for all of us. Our entire reality has been manipulated. The higher fuel prices, inflation, and increased housing expenses are all to bring the masses of people under one world authority.

The ungodly owns the Central Bank, the media, the education system, and the world leaders. What's being done in Ukraine with bombs is being done here in America with more subtle means. America is efficiently killing and removing its citizens. The enemy of all people is the state. This is the reason that governments around the world pushed for vaccinations. Those vaccinations are poison. The governments of all nations have effectively removed 50% of the world's population. The media has been so effective in warping our reality that most of us missed the Rapture. The people are already gone. Most won't realize what has happened until millions more are gone and we have reached the point of no return. We likely already have.

> **15 Beware of false prophets, which come to you in sheep's clothing, but inwardly they are ravening wolves.**
>
> **16 Ye shall know them by their fruits. Do men gather grapes of thorns, or figs of thistles?**
>
> **17 Even so every good tree bringeth forth good fruit; but a corrupt tree bringeth forth evil fruit.**
>
> **18 A good tree cannot bring forth evil fruit, neither can a corrupt tree bring forth good fruit.**
>
> **19 Every tree that bringeth not forth good fruit is hewn down, and cast into the fire.**
>
> **20 Wherefore by their fruits ye shall know them. (Mt 7:15-20 KJV)**

Freedom

We as Americans have a misconception about freedom. The enemy has slowly redefined what freedom means. Freedom no longer means liberty to pursue life, free of any pressure from state coercion, influence, and control. What we are now witnessing is a gradual erosion of values, freedom of speech, and a reduction in choices. All children are given the same state-appointed curriculum, whether the parents agree or not. Blacks and Whites marched for equality, and equality sounds good, but this is yet another trick of Satan. God's people are special, not equal.

> **For thou art an holy people unto the LORD thy God: the LORD thy God hath chosen thee to be a special people unto himself, above all people that are upon the face of the earth. (Deut 7:6 KJV)**

Americans who fought for equality had their hearts in the right place, but the Satanists and socialists do not have a problem with equality. In fact, they love it. They absolutely want all people who are obedient to the state to have their equal share. The problem, however, is no different than in the case of the man with one leg who asked the devil to make both his legs the same and now he has no legs.

The instructions in the OT Bible are so that God's people can live freely as "His" children. Once you go down the path of disobedience you are no longer a child of God, but you are rather a child of the state. Freedom for America has been redefined to simply mean, freedom to disobey God. Your earthly father, the state, will not tolerate any disobedience. Covid has given us a glimpse of the type of control that future American leaders are pursuing.

> *"In a country where the sole employer is the State, opposition means death by slow starvation. The old principle: who does not work shall not eat, has been replaced by a new one: who does not obey shall not eat."*
>
> – **Leon Trotsky**

Under socialism/communism private ownership of property will be relinquished to the state and the people who are under this system will not have a leg to stand on and will be required to lean on the state. If you do not think that this is possible here in America, history says otherwise. In May 1933, President Roosevelt required all Americans to turn in their gold and gold certificates in exchange for new monetary notes.

Nikita Krushchev in a speech given in 1962 to the Communist Party Congress stated that socialism will be victorious over capitalism not through fear or war, but by peace.

America has not only aborted its children, but we have also set aside our Bibles. Those things that you have discarded your enemies use and understand. They however use it as a tool against you, and they understand with proper miseducation, you won't really make sense of what's happening. The wisdom in the Bible is consistent. Through peace we're destroyed by deception, this is the Art of War.

> **And through his policy also he shall cause craft to prosper in his hand; and he shall magnify himself in his heart, and by peace shall destroy many: he shall also stand up against the Prince of princes; but he shall be broken without hand. (Dan 8:25 KJV)**

> *"Freedom is never more than one generation away from extinction. We didn't pass it to our children in the bloodstream. It must be fought for, protected, and handed on for them to do the same, or one day we will spend our sunset years telling our children and our children's children what it was once like in the United States where men were free."*

– **Ronald Reagan**

How Did It Happen?

Many of our children are being sold on the idea of socialism because capitalism doesn't seem to work. The disparity between those who have and those who don't is growing. It is estimated that the wealthiest 100 Whites have more wealth than the entire Black population. How did this happen?

After the freeing of slaves in 1865 from physical bondage, Blacks in some regions of America began to accumulate wealth. Segregation laws, contrary to what has been taught, actually benefited Blacks. Those who argue against segregation simply do not understand the monetary aspects of segregation vs. integration. Segregation which the Bible teaches, allowed Blacks, who continued to work in large numbers for Whites post-slavery, to only spend their money among the Black community. The money in places like Tulsa, OK, known historically as Black Wall Street, changed hands over 100 times within the community before leaving. Enriching this community and others like it in America.

So how do you destroy the wealth of a community or a nation? You employ *Art of War* tactics and enlist the services of loyal socialists to promote the idea of integration. The NAACP of yesterday is no different than the communist BLM group today (Black Lives Matter). The leadership of Martin Luther King and the Black church misled millions of Blacks down the path to where we are today because they also didn't know what will happen next.

After integration, the wealth that circulated within the community was lost. The money flowed out of the community, and the businesses and jobs followed. Instead of a community that was beginning to grow its wealth, it has now become a community dependent on state and local government. Black America has now become a community whose largest employer is the state and is dependent on federal housing and subsidies.

America's Black communities are already living under a socialist system. So what many American Socialists believe to be a failure of capitalism is not a failure of capitalism at all. Though America has gotten the closest to the ideal, true capitalism has never been experienced by those who are alive today. No Socialists have ever truly experienced capitalism, especially since the abandoning of the Gold Standard. Most of us today have never held a dollar that was attached to a God Standard or what is better known as a Gold Standard. The God standard is real wealth, something tangible as God created it. The centralization and *demon*etization of wealth by the Federal Reserve created the opportunity to print trillions of dollars and weaponize the money as needed.

Those who now control the money can make available easy credit and arbitrarily restrict the available flow of money and credit before recapturing the tangible wealth of its unknowing citizens.

The first attacks on America were focused on the Black community. Blacks and Whites have historically fought alongside one another in war, and the enemy of America has sought to destroy and divide the alliance of Whites and Blacks. What I've described is what integration was for the Black community. Globalization for America is integration by a different name. If you want to see America's future you need to look no further than the Black community.

"The best way to destroy the capitalist system is to debauch the currency."

-Vladimir Lenin

Communism

In March of 1937, Pope Pius XI delivered his *DIVINI REDEMPTORIS* to the Roman Catholic Church. In it he brought up his grave concerns about communism. I'll highlight some parts of it.

ENCYCLICAL OF POPE PIUS XI

ON ATHEISTIC COMMUNISM

TO THE PATRIARCHS, PRIMATES,

ARCHBISHOPS, BISHOPS, AND OTHER ORDINARIES

IN PEACE AND COMMUNION WITH THE APOSTOLIC SEE.

8 The Communism of today, more emphatically than similar movements in the past, **conceals in itself a false messianic idea**. A pseudo-ideal of justice, of equality, and fraternity in labor, impregnates all its doctrine and activity with a **deceptive mysticism,** which communicates a zealous and contagious enthusiasm to the multitudes entrapped by delusive promises. **This is especially true in an age like ours when unusual misery has resulted from the unequal distribution of the goods of this world.** This pseudo-ideal is even boastfully advanced as if it were responsible for certain economic progress. As a matter of fact, when such progress is at all real, its true

causes are quite different, for instance, the intensification of industrialism in countries which were formerly almost without it, the exploitation of immense natural resources, and the use of the most brutal methods to ensure the achievement of gigantic projects with a minimum of expense.

[9] The doctrine of modern Communism, which is often concealed under the most seductive trappings, is in substance based on the principles of dialectical and historical materialism previously advocated by Marx, of which the theoreticians of bolshevism claim to possess the only genuine interpretation. **According to this doctrine, there is in the world only one reality, matter**, the blind forces of which evolve into plant, animal, and man. Even human society is nothing but a phenomenon and form of matter, evolving in the same way. By a law of inexorable necessity and through a perpetual conflict of forces, **matter moves towards the final synthesis of a classless society.** In such a doctrine, as is evident, there is no room for the idea of God; there is no difference between matter and spirit, between soul and body; there is neither survival of the soul after death nor any hope in future life. Insisting on the dialectical aspect of their materialism, the Communists claim that the conflict which carries the world towards its final synthesis can be accelerated by man. Hence **they endeavor to sharpen the antagonisms which arise between the various classes of society. Thus the class struggle with its consequent violent hate and destruction takes on the aspects of a crusade for the progress of humanity.** On the other hand, all

other forces whatever, as long as they resist such systematic violence, must be annihilated as hostile to the human race.

[15] How is it possible that such a system, long since rejected scientifically and now proved erroneous by experience, how is it, We ask, that such a system could spread so rapidly in all parts of the world? The explanation lies in the fact that too few have been able to grasp the nature of Communism. **The majority instead succumb to its deception, skillfully concealed by the most extravagant promises. By pretending to desire only the betterment of the condition of the working classes**, by urging the removal of the very real abuses chargeable to the liberalistic economic order, and by demanding more equitable distribution of this world's goods (objectives entirely and undoubtedly legitimate), the Communist takes advantage of the present world-wide economic crisis to draw into the sphere of his influence even those sections of the populace which on principle reject all forms of materialism and terrorism. And as every error contains its element of truth, the partial truths to which We have referred are astutely presented according to the needs of time and place, to conceal, when convenient, the repulsive crudity and inhumanity of Communistic principles and tactics. Thus the Communist ideal wins over many of the better-minded members of the community. These in turn become the apostles of the movement among the younger intelligentsia who are still too immature to recognize the intrinsic errors of the system. **The preachers of Communism are also**

> **proficient in exploiting racial antagonisms and political divisions and oppositions.** They take advantage of the lack of orientation characteristic of modern agnostic science to burrow into the universities, where they bolster the principles of their doctrine with pseudo-scientific arguments.
>
> 16 If we would explain the blind acceptance of Communism by so many thousands of workmen, we must remember that the way had been already prepared for it by the religious and moral destitution in which wage-earners had been left by liberal economics. Even on Sundays and holy days, labor shifts were given no time to attend to their essential religious duties. No one thought of building churches within convenient distance of factories, nor of facilitating the work of the priest. On the contrary, laicism was actively and persistently promoted, with the result that we are now reaping the fruits of the errors so often denounced by Our Predecessors and by Ourselves. It can surprise no one that the Communistic fallacy should be spreading in a world already to a large extent de-Christianized.

While I don't agree with everything the Pope says and everything the Catholic Church does, Pope Pius was on the money on several aspects of Communism. I do fear that his main issue is that the state, and not himself and the Catholic Church are pulling the strings.

But he makes some prescient points. He says communism is rooted in a false messianic idea, a pseudo mysticism. There is a half-truth in communism that sounds right until you see it played out. The half-truth is that we should care about our brotherman. This is of course true. Believers of the Old and New Testaments will have no trouble regarding generosity and care for others as a quality desired by God of his children.

So what is the problem with communism? The problem is that this generosity is forced. By whom? A man with a gun. Who is this man? Whoever is at the top of the government. In Cuba, it is Diaz-Canal (after Castro). In Venezuela, it is Maduro (after Chavez). In Russia, it is Putin (after a list of leaders starting with Lenin), in China, it is Jinping (after Jintau and back to Mau), and in North Korea, it is Kim Jong-un.

Someone decides how much of your stuff should go to someone else. You belong to the state and the man at the top with the gun. One group is pitted against another and individual rights are non-existent.

God's design continues to reveal itself in all things. A centralized government and a single source of resources are in opposition to God and His design. Everything we need to live independently is possible, but man is afraid of independence, so he looks for a "Superman," a "philosopher king" to rule him.

The Israelites had God alone for their king, and yet even they wanted to have a king so they could be like all the other nations.

> **8 And it came to pass, when Samuel was old, that he made his sons judges over Israel.**
>
> **2 Now the name of his firstborn was Joel; and the name of his second, Abiah: they were judges in Beersheba.**

3 And his sons walked not in his ways, but turned aside after lucre, and took bribes, and perverted judgment.

4 Then all the elders of Israel gathered themselves together, and came to Samuel unto Ramah,

5 And said unto him, Behold, thou art old, and thy sons walk not in thy ways: now make us a king to judge us like all the nations.

6 But the thing displeased Samuel, when they said, Give us a king to judge us. And Samuel prayed unto the Lord.

7 And the Lord said unto Samuel, Hearken unto the voice of the people in all that they say unto thee: for they have not rejected thee, but they have rejected me, that I should not reign over them.

8 According to all the works which they have done since the day that I brought them up out of Egypt even unto this day, wherewith they have forsaken me, and served other gods, so do they also unto thee.

9 Now therefore hearken unto their voice: howbeit yet protest solemnly unto them, and shew them the manner of the king that shall reign over them.

10 And Samuel told all the words of the Lord unto the people that asked of him a king.

11 And he said, This will be the manner of the king that shall reign over you: He will take your sons, and appoint them for

himself, for his chariots, and to be his horsemen; and some shall run before his chariots.

12 And he will appoint him captains over thousands, and captains over fifties; and will set them to ear his ground, and to reap his harvest, and to make his instruments of war, and instruments of his chariots.

13 And he will take your daughters to be confectionaries, and to be cooks, and to be bakers.

14 And he will take your fields, and your vineyards, and your oliveyards, even the best of them, and give them to his servants.

15 And he will take the tenth of your seed, and of your vineyards, and give to his officers, and to his servants.

16 And he will take your menservants, and your maidservants, and your goodliest young men, and your asses, and put them to his work.

17 He will take the tenth of your sheep: and ye shall be his servants.

18 And ye shall cry out in that day because of your king which ye shall have chosen you; and the Lord will not hear you in that day.

19 Nevertheless the people refused to obey the voice of Samuel; and they said, Nay; but we will have a king over us;

20 That we also may be like all the nations; and that our king may judge us, and go out before us, and fight our battles.

> **[21] And Samuel heard all the words of the people, and he rehearsed them in the ears of the Lord.**
>
> **[22] And the Lord said to Samuel, Hearken unto their voice, and make them a king. And Samuel said unto the men of Israel, Go ye every man unto his city. (1 Sam 8:1-21 KJV).**

Samuel was a great man and a great leader, but he had one fatal flaw. He did not raise his sons right. He appointed them priests and judges, and they were worthless. The people had the right conclusion, but the wrong solution. They wanted a king to rule them.

God had created us for freedom. He wants to be our only king, but humans crave a leader who will take responsibility for them. Samuel was distraught because he knew what was happening, but God says, "give them what they want, but warn them." A king will:

- ⊙ Take their sons for his army (111-12),
- ⊙ Subjugate their daughters (13),
- ⊙ Seize their lands and businesses for himself (14-17).

This is just what communist leaders do *for the good of the people.* And the people love it. They are terrified by the call on every image bearer of God. They are terrified of *not* being just like everyone else (20). They want someone else to "go out before us and fight our battles."

Those few who don't want to be ruled want to rule. Those philosopher kings. Today, even in America, we can't even fish without a license. Lest we point to Russia, China, and Venezuela and ask, "What's wrong with them?" We must look at our own country and see how we are becoming just like them.

No new creation comes from communists. Without freedom of mind, there is no creation. Without freedom of the body, there is no freedom of mind. Those things that have shaped the world have come free from the free world: electricity, lights, refrigeration, cars, and mass production. Free men have innovated and given through the marketplace to those who valued their creations. The free men were rewarded for their efforts. That's what happens in a free economy.

Communism has done nothing to advance Man. China's great contribution to the world was gunpowder. But now, China's game plan is to steal innovations from free countries and produce them cheaply in state-owned factories.

Two types of people— those who believe in democracy, freedom, and religion and those who believe in communism, slavery, and atheism.

> It [Communism] is not new. It is, in fact, man's second oldest faith. Its promise was whispered in the first days of the Creation under the Tree of the Knowledge of Good and Evil: "Ye shall be as gods." It is the great alternative faith of mankind. Like all great faiths, its force derives from a simple vision. Other ages have had great visions. They have always been different versions of the same vision: the vision of God and man's relationship to God. The Communist vision is the vision of Man without God.
>
> It is the vision of man's mind displacing God as the creative intelligence of the world. It is the vision of man's liberated mind, by the sole force of its rational intelligence, redirecting man's destiny and reorganizing man's life and the world. It is the vision of man, once more the central

figure of the Creation, not because God made man in his image, but because man's mind makes him the most intelligent of the animals. Copernicus and his successors displaced man as the central fact of the universe by proving that the earth was not the central star of the universe. Communism restores man to his sovereignty by the simple method of denying God.

— Whittaker Chambers, *Witness*

Chapter 9

How to Change the World

So then how do we, who know what we know, change the world? There is only one thing that will change the world: The fear of God.

Fear

> **"The fear of the LORD is the beginning of wisdom: and the knowledge of the holy is understanding" (Prov 9:10).**

The Bible is able to foretell how the enemy will destroy God's children because our ancestors and the beast understand God's design. The beast's tactics are most effective during peace rather than during the traditional war. The truth in this is that you're always at war. You're either engaged in a traditional war or a war by deception.

The meaning of peace is the absence of opposition to socialism.

-Karl Marx

Why does the beast prefer deception?

The beast understands that God's people are guaranteed victory. As long as God is with you, your enemy can't defeat you in battle. So then everything that God orders you not to do, the beast must persuade you to do, which is --eat from the tree of knowledge--. Once you've eaten from this tree, God's protection is removed and like Adam and Eve, you're now naked, which is vulnerable. God's warning is that on that day you shall know death. One day for God and Heaven is 1000 years for man.

Leviticus 26:6-8 KJV

And I will give peace in the land, and ye shall lie down, and none shall make you afraid: and I will rid evil beasts out of the land, neither shall the sword go through your land. [7] And ye shall chase your enemies, and they shall fall before you by the sword. [8] And five of you shall chase an hundred, and an hundred of you shall put ten thousand to flight: and your enemies shall fall before you by the sword.

Isaiah 59:1-4 KJV

Behold, the LORD'S hand is not shortened, that it cannot save; neither his ear heavy, that it cannot hear: [2] But your iniquities have separated between you and your God, and your sins have hid his face from you, that he will not hear. [3] For your hands are defiled with blood, and your fingers with iniquity; your lips have spoken lies, your tongue hath muttered perverseness. [4] None calleth for justice, nor any pleadeth for truth: they trust in vanity, and speak lies; they conceive mischief, and bring forth iniquity.

Joshua 7:10-12 KJV

And the LORD said unto Joshua, Get thee up; wherefore liest thou thus upon thy face? [11] Israel hath sinned, and they have also transgressed my covenant which I commanded them: for they have even taken of the accursed thing, and have also stolen, and dissembled also, and they have put it even among their own stuff. [12] Therefore the children of Israel could not stand before their enemies, but turned their backs before their enemies, because they were accursed: neither will I be with you any more, except ye destroy the accursed from among you.

Proverbs 14:12 KJV

There is a way which seemeth right unto a man, but the end thereof are the ways of death.

Truth protects you from deception and children in abundance protect you from invasion. Numbers are so important that it's actually a book in our Bible. The command to be fruitful and multiply is a military strategy, because of course, there are strengths in numbers. The two commands of being fruitful and multiply and not eating the tree keep your enemy from encroaching on the minds and land of God's people.

What we have done now is disobey both laws and we're now witnessing a downward trajectory of both life and liberty. God's people are not to live among the Godless, globalization and a one world order are in opposition to God.

History proves these points to be true. The Native American introduction to foreign people, the Mayan introduction to the Spanish, and the Africans welcoming Europeans. None of these past interactions with foreign nations ended well for the native populations. The Tasmanian people are now extinct and King Leopold III killed an estimated 20 million Africans in the Congo. Now today America shakes hands and trades with communist nations. Whenever you have different people, religions, or cultures trying to live among one another, that's not integration, it's war. You have now created a hostile environment where one idea, culture, or people must press upon the other a conflicting culture until one subdues the other.

This is the environment we live in today. America is becoming more and more hostile to God's people. The ideas of the secular in our society are influencing schools, media, and politics and anyone who speaks in opposition is threatened with being canceled. Cancel culture is communism and currently, the only free speech being tolerated is by those that are for feminism and the gay community. God's people have failed in maintaining an environment where those who have a religion can feel comfortable enough to disagree with ideas that are in opposition to their beliefs.

It is the enemies of God's people who introduce these ideas because they fear your God, the fear that God's people are to possess. The reverence that the beast shows for your God, isn't present among those who claim to be men and women of God. The beast absolutely understands who we are and knows that God is real. Those men and women whom they persuade to live and promote their ideas are merely tools to be discarded once their objective is met.

"[T]he useful idiots, the leftists who are idealistically believing in the beauty of the Soviet socialist or Communist or whatever system, when they get disillusioned, they become the worst enemies. That's why my KGB instructors specifically made the point: never bother with leftists. Forget about these political prostitutes. Aim higher. [...] They serve a purpose only at the stage of destabilization of a nation. For example, your leftists in the United States: all these professors and all these beautiful civil rights defenders. They are instrumental in the process of subversion only to destabilize a nation. When their job is completed, they are not needed anymore. They know too much. Some of them, when they get disillusioned, when they see that Marxist-Leninists come to power—obviously they get offended—they think that they will come to power. That will never happen, of course. They will be lined up against the wall and shot."

-Yuri Bezmenov

No one trusts a traitor and why would they? How can anyone trust those who would not only betray their people but disobey God? The war manual we call the Bible outlines the punishment for treason. The Bible is God's (UCMJ) Uniformed Code of Military Justice, which outlines how those who are part of his Army are to conduct themselves and the punishments for those transgressions.

Deuteronomy 17:2-5 KJV

If there be found among you, within any of thy gates which the LORD thy God giveth thee, man or woman, that hath wrought wickedness in the sight of the LORD thy God, in transgressing his covenant, [3] And hath gone and served other gods, and worshipped them, either the sun, or moon, or any of the host of heaven, which I have not commanded; [4] And it be

told thee, and thou hast heard of it, and enquired diligently, and, behold, it be true, and the thing certain, that such abomination is wrought in Israel: [5] Then shalt thou bring forth that man or that woman, which have committed that wicked thing, unto thy gates, even that man or that woman, and shalt stone them with stones, till they die.

God's children are to fear the Almighty, which is to have a reverence for his authority. This respect for God's authority is displayed by the beast, which is why he uses deception and seeks to avoid a traditional war.

Deuteronomy 11:22-28 KJV

For if ye shall diligently keep all these commandments which I command you, to do them, to love the LORD your God, to walk in all his ways, and to cleave unto him; [23] Then will the LORD drive out all these nations from before you, and ye shall possess greater nations and mightier than yourselves. [24] Every place whereon the soles of your feet shall tread shall be yours: from the wilderness and Lebanon, from the river, the river Euphrates, even unto the uttermost sea shall your coast be. [25] There shall no man be able to stand before you: for the LORD your God shall lay the fear of you and the dread of you upon all the land that ye shall tread upon, as he hath said unto you. [26] Behold, I set before you this day a blessing and a curse; [27] A blessing, if ye obey the commandments of the LORD your God, which I command you this day: [28] And a curse, if ye will not obey the commandments of the LORD your God, but turn aside out of the way which I command you this day, to go after other gods, which ye have not known.

You are to choose whom you are to follow. If you don't fear God you will fear the beast, If you don't follow God's law you will follow the beast's laws of communism. Under communism, fear is the tool that keeps billions who are already under communism silent. This fear will paralyze you to move or act. The beast will become your God and disobedience will not be tolerated.

It's the responsibility of God's people to prepare their children for war by deception. If we forego our responsibility to educate, discipline and create an environment that not only protects our children physically but mentally, we can blame no one other than ourselves.

It is these things that establish the Bible as a war manual and not a love story. Again the greatest gift our ancestors can give us is 'Truth' and that manifests itself as life and liberty.

Another condition of integration is the death and disease that follows. This is true of the Mayan civilization, Native Americans, and Europeans when they entered Africa. History notes that many of these people were devastated by the diseases that were introduced as a result of the transplanted foreigners. History repeats itself today and now we're experiencing a global pandemic in a global economy. Now the leaders who pushed for globalization advise that the best way to stop the spread is to do what God commanded. Of course, they won't use those words, but they advise we stay away from one another. However, if we take a closer look at history we then realize it's the Satanists that we're to remain separate from. It's those who came to kill and pillage that brought with them death and disease.

God's design is true down to the creation of his animal world. The different species that god has created, each has its place on Earth, and the introduction of one species to another region on Earth disrupts that ecosystem and the life of other animals that depend on that environment's systems.

Another tool of your enemy is fear. Once you accept the doctrine of love, you put down your weapons. Once you accept the fear presented by your enemy, you have now put down your faith in God. It is the Creator who said he would protect you from all things. This is your covenant with the Almighty.

Exodus 19:5

> **Now therefore, if ye will obey my voice indeed, and keep my covenant, then ye shall be a peculiar treasure unto me above all people: for all the earth is mine:**

Exodus 23:25 KJV

> **And ye shall serve the LORD your God, and he shall bless thy bread, and thy water; and I will take sickness away from the midst of thee.**

Deuteronomy 7:15 KJV

> **And the LORD will take away from thee all sickness, and will put none of the evil diseases of Egypt, which thou knowest, upon thee; but will lay them upon all them that hate thee.**

The change in culture from Godly to Godless is gradual. We've been moved from a Godly civilization to modern barbarism. It is fear that is used to silence the Godly, it is fear that motivated many to stay away from church and family and it is fear that persuaded many to take the vaccination.

> *There are, besides, eternal truths, such as Freedom, etc., that are common to all states of society. But Communism abolishes eternal truths, it abolishes all religion, and all morality, instead of constituting them on a new basis; it, therefore, acts in contradiction to all past historical experience.*
>
> — *Karl Marx*

God gives you free will and the devil gives you bad choices

If there is anything more valuable than life, it would be freedom. To have life without freedom is death. This is why many throughout history have chosen to risk their lives to obtain or maintain freedom. This is the intent of God's law so that his children will not fall to their enemies. Contrary to what many may believe, your sins are not forgiven. Your sins are punishable in life before death. Those who are most vulnerable are those who will typically fall prey to your enemies first. Those being your children and your elders. God's punishment is built into his design, as is his reward.

> *"If you had not committed great sins, God would not have sent a punishment like me upon you."*
>
> **-Genghis Khan**

The world looks the way it does not because of the acts of the godless, but because of the inactivity of the godly. God's design of the world is that all things have an opposition. God's people have failed to defend and protect his women and children, "It is quoted that the greatest deterrent for war is preparation for war."

> "If you want peace, prepare for war" comes from the book "*Epitoma Rei Militaris,*"

That's the purpose of being fruitful and multiplying. Life in abundance, children, and family, is the foundation of a nation. God's design is for races and tribes within races to live separately from one another. Forcing different groups of people together creates more division and hostility instead of unity. This is why there is so much death on the streets in America. People are to live among those who are not only of the same race but have the same beliefs. Those who worship the same God. Our communities are failing and our marriages are failing because we live in opposition to God's law. Living separately doesn't mean we can't coexist, it's respecting those differences and allowing those who choose to live differently to do so.

An example of this would be how the Amish communities have made a conscious decision to live separately from others. These communities continue to interact with those communities around them in commerce but live only among those who wish to live the way they do. What's interesting is that you do not hear of mass shootings, school shootings, and obscene levels of violence among these groups. This is how God's people are to live. The Amish do not force their lifestyle on others and we're not supposed to force upon anyone our ideas on their communities. Integration is a tool of communism, which allows for the godless to live among the godly. This is the deception that Blacks in America accepted and this is why the Black communities in America look the way they do. Blacks are not only supposed to live among Blacks but they are also supposed to separate themselves again from those who choose to live in opposition to their beliefs. Contrary to what history says, many Blacks did not want integration. This is also what the White population is also supposed to do. Whites are not only to separate themselves from Blacks but Whites who do not worship as they do.

If you want the answer to how you stop school shootings and the high levels of violence that exist on the streets in America, there's your answer. All the answers to what's wrong with the world are in the Bible. The violence that exists in Chicago streets is simply because the people who police the streets of South Chicago do not live there. Blacks are supposed to police Black communities, this would considerably reduce if not end the senseless shootings of unarmed Blacks by White cops by limiting the interaction of these two groups. This will actually unite Whites and Blacks instead of divide, which is what the enemy of Blacks and Whites has achieved. Yes, Blacks and Whites have the same enemy. The enemy of all God's people is Satanists. This is the force in America and the world that is pushing Godless ideas and promoting values that divide people.

What God's people are to do is to divide themselves the way they choose. If God's people do not divide themselves, then the Godless will divide you. This is the current condition of America, the Satanic have divided us by race, gender, religion, age, wealth, and political affiliation. Under this division, all groups and all people are losing their freedoms. God's people who choose to group themselves, although separate, are supposed to be allies of one another to maintain the freedoms of everyone. Although the Satanic have divided us into these groups to fight among one another, the Satanists still remain among them.

That is the point of God's people dividing themselves, so that they may live the way they choose and rid themselves of the weeds among them. The Satanists use integration to influence the behavior of all people, it's so that they may teach your children ideas that are in opposition to your beliefs. It allows for them to sow tares among your wheat.

Matthew 13:38 KJV

> **The field is the world; the good seed are the children of the kingdom; but the tares are the children of the wicked one;**

What history teaches is that everybody doesn't place the same value on life as others. When confronted by those who represent the devil, you'll be given the option of life in exchange for slavery. If you want freedom you must be willing to fight for that. Upon birth, every man has a right to Life and Liberty. Those who have fought and died for freedom understand its value. Those born under freedom at some point take their freedoms for granted.

The freedoms that you take for granted, are free speech, freedom of worship, to carry a weapon, and freedom of movement. You lose these freedoms as you move further away from God's law. The Satanist has confused the meaning of freedom. Freedom is truly the ability to live the way you choose within the framework of natural law, God's design. The natural laws of God maintain the freedom of all people without imposing on the freedoms of others.

The Satanist idea of freedom is the restriction of speech, weapons, worship, and movement. It may sound counterintuitive, but to accomplish this the Satanist only needs to give God's people more freedoms, and more choices. The idea is that if you give a man enough rope he'll hang himself. That rope is integration, homosexuality, abortion, and feminism. These ideas do what they're intended to do and that is to move God's people away from God's laws and natural order. While at the same time it increases violence by forcing different people and ideas together. It creates hostility and separation of groups who should be allies of one another. These ideas also reduce the number of God's children, which is also a primary goal of the Satanists.

However, in order to enslave the masses, Satanists must first change the meaning of freedom. Today what we call freedom is simply the ability to disobey God. Disobedience to God is not the idea of freedom the founding fathers had in mind when America was founded. Those so-called freedoms actually move you closer to slavery. Satanists create the problem and then offer a solution that moves you closer to Communism, Satan's government.

Like the Bible has done, you can predict what will happen next. Prayer, discipline, and allegiance to the flag were removed from American schools, what did we think would happen next? Fathers, structure, and discipline were removed from the Black community, what did we think would happen next? Homosexuality, feminism, and death, replaced family, structure, and moral values in our music and media, what did we think would happen next?

This is an example of one of the laws of physics, matter and anti-matter cannot occupy the same space and time. Our communities will either represent God or Satanists. You cannot maintain both within the same space and time. The group, the community, and the nation must choose whom, it'll represent.

You must always choose Life and God, free will. For when the devil offers you a choice, it'll be death or slavery, bad choices.

Appendix A

Prophets Of Satan

Words from Communist – slavery, and atheism

The goal of your enemy is outlined in the book, *The Art of War*, which says, "the supreme art of war is defeating your enemy without fighting."

> *"Freedom in capitalist society always remains about the same as it was in ancient Greek republics: Freedom for slave owners."*
>
> **-Vladimir Lenin**

> *"Despair is typical of those who do not understand the causes of evil, see no way out, and are incapable of struggle."*
>
> **-Vladimir Lenin**

> *"Communism is the riddle of history solved, and it knows itself to be this solution."*
>
> **-Karl Marx, Economic & Philosophic Manuscripts of 1844**

> *"You are horrified at our intending to do away with private property. But in your existing society, private property is already done away*

with for nine-tenths of the population; its existence for the few is solely due to its non-existence in the hands of those nine-tenths. You reproach us, therefore, with intending to do away with a form of property, the necessary condition for whose existence is the non-existence of any property for the immense majority of society.

In one word, you reproach us with intending to do away with your property. Precisely so: that is just what we intend."

-Karl Marx, The Communist Manifesto

"[T]he useful idiots, the leftists who are idealistically believing in the beauty of the Soviet socialist or Communist or whatever system, when they get disillusioned, they become the worst enemies. That's why my KGB instructors specifically made the point: never bother with leftists. Forget about these political prostitutes. Aim higher. [...] They serve a purpose only at the stage of destabilization of a nation. For example, your leftists in the United States: all these professors and all these beautiful civil rights defenders. They are instrumental in the process of subversion only to destabilize a nation. When their job is completed, they are not needed anymore. They know too much. Some of them, when they get disillusioned, when they see that Marxist-Leninists come to power—obviously they get offended—they think that they will come to power. That will never happen, of course. They will be lined up against the wall and shot."

-Yuri Bezmenov

"In a country where the sole employer is the State, opposition means death by slow starvation. The old principle: who does not work shall not eat, has been replaced by a new one: who does not obey shall not eat."

-Leon Trotsky

When we hang the capitalists they will sell us the rope we use.

-Joseph Stalin

It's not the people who vote that count. It's the people who count the votes.

-Joseph Stalin

Great Britain provided time; the United States provided money and Soviet Russia provided blood.

-Joseph Stalin

By May, 1st, 1937, there should not be one single church left within the borders of Soviet Russia, and the idea of God will have been banished from the Soviet Union as a remnant of the Middle Ages, which has been used for the purpose of oppressing the working classes.

-Joseph Stalin

It doesn't matter who they vote for, they always vote for us.

-Joseph Stalin

[American Communist Party] legally exists in the U.S.A., it nominates its candidates in the elections, including Presidential elections.

-Joseph Stalin

Everybody has a right to be stupid, but some people abuse the privilege.

-Joseph Stalin

The press must grow day in and day out - it is our Party's sharpest and most powerful weapon.

~ Joseph Stalin

The goal of socialism is communism.

~Vladimir Lenin

The way to crush the bourgeoisie is to grind them between the millstones of taxation and inflation.

~Vladimir Lenin

Truth is the most precious thing. That's why we should ration it.

~Vladimir Lenin

People always have been and they always will be stupid victims of deceit and self-deception in politics.

~Vladimir Lenin

As an ultimate objective, "peace" simply means communist world control.

~Vladimir Lenin

Atheism is a natural and inseparable part of Marxism, of the theory and practice of scientific socialism. Our program necessarily includes the propaganda of atheism.

~Vladimir Lenin

The best way to control the opposition is to lead it ourselves.

~Vladimir Lenin

Germany will militarize herself out of existence, England will expand herself out of existence, and America will spend herself out of existence.

-Vladimir Lenin

The establishment of a central bank is 90% of communizing a nation.

-Vladimir Lenin

Give us the child for eight years and it will be a Bolshevik forever.

-Vladimir Lenin

There are no morals in politics; there is only expedience. A scoundrel may be of use to us just because he is a scoundrel.

-Vladimir Lenin

We are not shooting enough professors.

-Vladimir Lenin

There can be nothing more abominable than religion.

-Vladimir Lenin

The best way to destroy the capitalist system is to debauch the currency.

-Vladimir Lenin

The oppressed are allowed once every few years to decide which particular representatives of the oppressing class are to represent and repress them in parliament.

-Vladimir Lenin

It is true that liberty is precious; so precious that it must be carefully rationed.

-Vladimir Lenin

Of all the arts, for us, the cinema is the most important.

-Vladimir Lenin

When it comes to hang the capitalists they will compete with each other to sell us the rope at a lower price.

-Vladimir Lenin

Atheism is the natural and inseparable part of Communism.

-Vladimir Lenin

By destroying the peasant economy and driving the peasant from the country to the town, the famine creates a proletariat... Furthermore, the famine can and should be a progressive factor not only economically. It will force the peasant to reflect on the bases of the capitalist system, demolish faith in the tsar and tsarism, and consequently in due course make the victory of the revolution easier... Psychologically all this talk about feeding the starving and so on essentially reflects the usual sugary sentimentality of our intelligentsia.

-Vladimir Lenin

Fascism is capitalism in decay.

-Vladimir Lenin

Capitalists will sell us the rope we will hang them with.

-Vladimir Lenin

Our program necessarily includes the propaganda of atheism.

-Vladimir Lenin

When a liberal is abused, he says, 'Thank God they didn't beat me.' When he is beaten, he thanks God they didn't kill him. When he is killed, he will thank God that his immortal soul has been delivered from its mortal clay.

-Vladimir Lenin

We have no compassion and we ask no compassion from you. When our turn comes, we shall not make excuses for the terror.

-Karl Marx

The theory of Communism may be summed up in one sentence: Abolish all private property.

-Karl Marx

Catch a man a fish, and you can sell it to him. Teach a man to fish, and you ruin a wonderful business opportunity.

-Karl Marx

The meaning of peace is the absence of opposition to socialism.

-Karl Marx

The democratic concept of man is false because it is Christian. The democratic concept holds that . . . each man is a sovereign being. This is the illusion, dream, and postulate of Christianity.

-Karl Marx

There are, besides, eternal truths, such as Freedom, etc., that are common to all states of society. But Communism abolishes eternal truths, it abolishes all religion, and all morality, instead of constituting them on a new basis; it, therefore, acts in contradiction to all past historical experience.

-Karl Marx

A heavy or progressive or graduated income tax is necessary for the proper development of Communism.

-Karl Marx

The first requisite for the happiness of the people is the abolition of religion.

-Karl Marx

The Jews of Poland are the smeariest of all races.

-Karl Marx

Anyone who knows anything of history knows that great social changes are impossible without feminine upheaval. Social progress can be measured exactly by the social position of the fair sex, the ugly ones included.

-Karl Marx

Owners of capital will stimulate working class to buy more and more of expensive goods, houses, and technology, pushing them to take more and more expensive credits until their debt becomes unbearable. The unpaid debt will lead to bankruptcy of banks which will have to be nationalized and State will have to take the road which will eventually lead to communism.

-Karl Marx

I wish to avenge myself against the One who rules above.

-Karl Marx

To destroy Christianity, we must first destroy the British Empire.

-Karl Marx

Religion is the sigh of the oppressed creature, the heart of a heartless world, and the soul of soulless conditions. It is the opium of the people.

-Karl Marx

"Private property has made us so stupid and partial that an object is only ours when we have it when it exists for us as capital ... Thus all the physical and intellectual senses have been replaced by ... the sense of having."

-Karl Marx

"Social progress can be measured exactly by the social position of the fair sex."

-Karl Marx

"They don't know it, but they are doing it."

-Karl Marx

"A nation that enslaves another forges its own chains."

-Karl Marx

"In a country where the sole employer is the State, opposition means death by slow starvation. The old principle: who does not work shall not eat, has been replaced by a new one: who does not obey shall not eat."

-Leon Trotsky

"Religions are illogical primitive ignorance. There is nothing as ridiculous and tragic as a religious government."

-Leon Trotsky

"The dictatorship of the Communist Party is maintained by recourse to every form of violence."

-Leon Trotsky

"The pillars of Hercules of the United States are vulgarity and stupidity."

-Leon Trotsky

"The people will have the right to elect their representatives from a list of candidates [who have been approved by the Party]."

-Leon Trotsky

"You are starving? This is not famine yet! When your women start eating their children, then you may come and say we are starving".

-Leon Trotsky

"If for the sake of Communism it is necessary for us to destroy 9/10ths of the people, we must not hesitate".

-Vladimir Lenin

"First of all, we have to understand what communism is, the Soviet communism, is basically a mask for Bolshevism, which is a mask for Judaism."

-Bobby Fischer

"There is much in the fact of Bolshevism itself, in the fact that so many Jews are Bolshevists, in the fact that the ideals of Bolshevism at many points are consonant with the finest ideals of Judaism."

-The Jewish Chronicle, 4/4/19

"Without Jews, there would never have been Bolshevism. For a Jew, nothing is more insulting than the truth. The bloodthirsty Jewish terrorists have murdered sixty-six million in Russia from 1918 to 1957.".

-Aleksandr Solzhenitsyn (1918-2008), Nobel Peace Prize Winner and Patriot

"Every Jew who is sincerely interested in the plight of the Jews... should realize that the best sons of the Jewish people are the Jewish Communists and that the most faithful ally of the Jews... is the Communist Party".

-"Anti-Semitism Must be Defeated" Jewish Life of New York, Issue May 1938"

"First of all, we have to understand what communism is, the Soviet communism, is basically a mask for Bolshevism, which is a mask for Judaism.".

-Bobby Fischer

"The world revolution which we will experience will be exclusively our affair and will rest in our hands. This revolution will tighten the Jewish domination over all other people".

-Paris Jewish Magazine "Peuple Juif" Feb 8th, 1919

"If you wish to be a success in the world, promise everything, deliver nothing."

-Napoleon Bonaparte

"The best way to make everyone poor is to insist on equality of wealth."

-Napoleon Bonaparte

"You don't reason with intellectuals. You shoot them."

-Napoleon Bonaparte

"The purpose of religion is to keep the poor from killing the rich."

-Napoleon Bonaparte

"If I were to give liberty to the press, my power could not last three days."

-Napoleon Bonaparte

"A woman laughing is a woman conquered."

-Napoleon Bonaparte

"Terrorism, War & Bankruptcy are caused by the privatization of money, issued as a debt and compounded by interest."

-Napoleon Bonaparte

"I fear three newspapers more than a hundred thousand bayonets."

-Napoleon Bonaparte

"When a government is dependent upon bankers for money, they and not the leaders of the government control the situation"

-Napoleon Bonaparte

"Power is what they like - it is the greatest of all aphrodisiacs."

-Napoleon Bonaparte

"Medicine is a collection of uncertain prescriptions, the results of which, taken collectively, are more fatal than useful to mankind."

-Napoleon Bonaparte

"Fools have a great advantage over the wise; they are always self-satisfied."

-Napoleon Bonaparte

"Governments keep their promises only when they are forced, or when it is to their advantage to do so."

-Napoleon Bonaparte

"The fool has one great advantage over a man of sense; he is always satisfied with himself."

-Napoleon Bonaparte

"History is written by the winners."

-Napoleon Bonaparte

"The world suffers a lot. Not because the violence of bad people. But because of the silence of the good people."

-Napoleon Bonaparte

"The Jews are the master robbers of the modern age."

-Napoleon Bonaparte

"When people cease to complain, they cease to think."

-Napoleon Bonaparte

"The reason most people fail instead of succeed is they trade what they want most for what they want at the moment."

-Napoleon Bonaparte

"The World is not ruined by the wickedness of the wicked, but by the weakness of the good."

-Napoleon Bonaparte

"History is a set of lies agreed upon."

-Napoleon Bonaparte

"There is no need to exaggerate the part played in the creation of Bolshevism and in the actual bringing about of the Russian Revolution, by these international and for the most part, atheistical Jews; it is certainly a very great one; it probably outweighs all others. With the notable exception of Lenin, the majority of the leading figures are Jews. Moreover, the principal inspiration and driving power come from the Jewish leaders".

-Winston Churchill

WORDS FROM DEMOCRACY

– *Freedom, and Religion*

"How do you tell a Communist? Well, it's someone who reads Marx and Lenin. And how do you tell an anti-Communist? It's someone who understands Marx and Lenin."

-Ronald Reagan

"Civil government, so far as it is instituted for the security of property, is in reality instituted for the defense of the rich against the poor, or of those who have some property against those who have none at all."

-Adam Smith

"Socialism is an alternative to capitalism as potassium cyanide is an alternative to water."

-Ludwig von Mises, Human Action: A Treatise on Economics

"The difference between communism and socialism is that under socialism central planning ends with a gun in your face, whereas under communism central planning begins with a gun in your face."

-Kevin D. Williamson, The Politically Incorrect Guide to Socialism

"Loyalty and Obedience always look like Love. Love doesn't always look like Loyalty and Obedience."

-James Taylor

"I freed a thousand slaves, I could have freed a thousand more if only they knew they were slaves."

-Harriet Tubman

"We could have been victorious if I could have convinced Blacks we were at war."

-James Taylor

"There are only two types of people in the world, builders and destroyers."

-James Dubose

"There are only two types of people in the world, builders and destroyers. Builders make everyone around them better and destroyers eventually destroy themselves after they have destroyed everyone around them."

-James Dubose

"Not any man can draw the word out of the sword and not any man can draw the sword out of the word."

-James Taylor

"The mark of the beast is anything that is not the mark of God."

-James Taylor

"Liberation from your man, Liberation from your family, and Liberation from your God."

-James Dubose

"Liberation is the freedom to make the wrong decision."

-James Dubose

"We are not waiting on God. God is waiting on us."

-James Dubose

"Give a man too much freedom and he will destroy himself."

-Unknown

"All warfare is based on deception."

--Sun Tzu, The Art of War

"It's far easier to convince your enemy to abort a million soldiers than to face ten million soldiers on the battlefield."

-James Taylor

"There's no such thing as an Atheist. If you don't believe in God, one will be appointed to you. Therefore, you can choose it but you can't use it.

-James Taylor

Never leave success to chance.

-James Taylor

Communism overtly denounces God, Capitalism covertly denounces God

-James Taylor

Definitions

Another tool we need to use is the power to define the words used to describe events, people, and places in the Bible. The Bible is written in such a way as to withstand the test of time. Its use of words is brilliant in that it understood that with the passing of time there would be little if any deviation from the meaning. So provided for you is a list of words as defined by Webster Merriam that you'll need to reference back to as you read the Bible. For the purpose and ease of understanding, only the meaning that pertains to the Bible will be used. Most words have several meanings, some of which are not related to the discussion.

Beast: an unkind or cruel person; a person or thing of a particular kind

> **Now the serpent was more subtil than any beast of the field which the LORD God had made. And he said unto the woman, Yea, hath God said, Ye shall not eat of every tree of the garden? (Gen 3:1 KJV)**

Serpent: devil; a treacherous person

> **And the serpent said unto the woman, Ye shall not surely die (Gen 3:4 KJV)**

Lamb: an innocent, weak, or gentle person

Goat: a person who is blamed for a loss or a failure; a licentious man

> Note: the goat is used to represent those who worship the devil and also the head of the baphomet.

> **Then ye shall sacrifice one kid of the goats for a sin offering, and two lambs of the first year for a sacrifice of peace offerings (Lev 23:19 KJV).**

Naked: unarmed, defenseless

> **And they were both naked, the man and his wife, and were not ashamed (Gen 2:25 KJV).**

Covenant: contract; a usually formal, solemn, and binding agreement; compact

> **And I, behold, I establish my covenant with you, and with your seed after you (Gen 9:9 KJV).**

Curse: to bring great evil upon; afflict; evil or misfortune that comes as if in response to imprecation or as retribution

Law: a binding custom or practice of a community; a rule of conduct or action prescribed or formally recognized as binding or enforced by a controlling authority

> **One law and one manner shall be for you, and for the stranger that sojourneth with you (Nu 15:16 KJV).**

Sin: transgression of the law of God; a vitiated state of human nature in which the self is estranged from God.

> **And the LORD said unto Moses, Whosoever hath sinned against me, him will I blot out of my book (EX 32:33 KJV).**

Virgin: an absolutely chaste young woman; chaste; morally pure or decent; not sinful; free of impurity or stain; unsullied; not changed from a natural or original condition; not affected by human activity.

> **Therefore the Lord himself shall give you a sign; Behold, a virgin shall conceive, and bear a son, and shall call his name Immanuel (Isa 7:14 KJV).**

Belial: biblical name of the devil

> **Certain men, the children of Belial, are gone out from among you, and have withdrawn the inhabitants of their city, saying, Let us go and serve other gods, which ye have not known (Deut 13:13 KJV).**

Printed in Great Britain
by Amazon